MASTER THE BASICS:

SPANISH

by
Christopher Kendris
B.S., M.S., Columbia University in the City of New York
M.A., Ph.D., Northwestern University in Evanston, Illinois

Diplômé, Faculté des Lettres, Université de Paris et
Institut de Phonétique, Paris (en Sorbonne)

Formerly Assistant Professor, Department of French and
Spanish, State University of New York, Albany, New York

Barron's Educational Series, Inc.

To the sweet memory of my mother
and to the memory of my father

For St. Sophia Greek Orthodox Church
of Albany, New York, my parish,
and
For my three grandsons
Bryan, Daniel, Matthew
with love

All inquiries should be addressed to:
Barron's Educational Series, Inc.
250 Wireless Boulevard
Hauppauge, NY 11788

Library of Congress Catalog Card No. 87-1398
International Standard Book No. 0-8120-3763-4

Library of Congress Cataloging-in-Publication Data

Kendris, Christopher.
   Master the basics — Spanish.

   Includes index.
   1. Spanish language — Grammar — 1950-   . I. Title.
PC4112.5.K44   1987   468.2'421   87-1398
ISBN 0-8120-3763-4

PRINTED IN THE UNITED STATES OF AMERICA

456   9770   13 12 11 10

Contents

Preface

This is one of a new miniseries of language grammar reviews. This book is intended to help you brush up on your Spanish grammar for instant communication and comprehension because the original numerical arrangement gives you fast and easy access to what you need to know or verify.

Beginning on p. 1 there is a diagnostic test that you ought to take immediately. It consists of 60 questions. Three questions are taken from each of the 20 chapters, which are listed in the Table of Contents as §1. through §20. Take the test to find out what you know, what you don't know, and where your strengths and weaknesses are. An Answer Key and Explained Answers are at the end of the diagnostic test. There, you will also find an analysis of the question numbers and the § numbers. In this way, you can refer to particular § numbers where your answers were not correct and brush up where needed. The complete brush up section consists mainly of the Basics, the Parts of Speech, and Special Topics, all of which are outlined in detail in the Table of Contents.

Occasionally I offer some mnemonic tips (memory aids) to help you remember certain aspects of Spanish grammar and vocabulary. For example, if you cannot remember that the Spanish word for twenty (*veinte*) is spelled with *ei* or *ie,* remember it this way:

| Mnemonic tip | T W | E | N T Y |
| | *V* | *E* | *I N T E* |

Mnemonic devices are very useful in learning and remembering. Students learn and remember in different ways. What works for you may not work for someone else. You must think of ways to help yourself remember. If you think of a way that seems foolish, don't tell anyone. Just let it work for you. One of my students told me that she finally figured out a way to remember the meaning of *buscar* / to look for. She said, "I'm looking for a *bus* or a *car.*" How many can you make up? Here are a few more mnemonic tips. Some students confuse **hoy** and **hay.** See these pictures in your mind:

The pronunciation of *hay* is like the English word eye. You don't remember the Spanish word for eyes / *los ojos?!* Watch this:

And this:

| Mnemonic tip | A | Y | E R |
| | | Y | E S T E R D A Y |

If I have omitted anything you think is important, if you spot any misprints, or if you have any suggestions for the improvement of the next edition, please contact the publisher.

Christopher Kendris
B.S., M.S., M.A., Ph.D.

How to Use This Book

So that you can get the most out of *Master the Basics: Spanish,* follow these steps.

Step 1 The first thing to do is to become familiar with this book. Turn the pages and look at each page for a few seconds. When you reach the Contents, examine it carefully. If you find something that strikes your interest, turn to that section to see exactly what is there. Do you want to know when the subjunctive should be used? Fan the pages until you come to §7.6 — 18 or go straight to the page given in the Contents. I'm sure you will find §7.10 of special interest and value. Do not begin to do any studying until you have reviewed every page. It won't take more than about ten minutes.

Step 2 Take the diagnostic test, beginning on p. 3. At the end of that preliminary test, you will find the Explained Answers and a Diagnostic Analysis. Check the question numbers that you had right or wrong and, if wrong, turn to the appropriate section and study it, making certain you understand the explanations, so that you can learn more about that particular element of Spanish. And if you happen to have many answers right, do not assume that you know that particular element of Spanish thoroughly. Asking only three questions from each of the 20 sections is just to give you an idea of your strengths and weaknesses.

Step 3 The next step is to go through the entire Grammar Brush-Up, reviewing some portions and studying others in depth. The final part of this book is Let's Review. You can do the 200 exercises and activities in this section either after having done the Grammar Brush-Up or as you work through the book. The questions are keyed to the numerical reference system in the Brush-Up and the Answers sections. Another possibility is to do both: try the questions corresponding to each chapter after you have studied the chapter, and then to do them again for a final review after you have worked through the Brush-Up.

The Spanish-English vocabulary will be useful as you practice your Spanish and the Index provides an easy reference to any grammatical point that you may want to check.

Now begin with Step 1!

FIND OUT WHAT YOU KNOW

This diagnostic test will help put some touching up on your brushing-up. The test covers material presented in the Basics, the Parts of Speech, and Special Topics, all of which are included in §1. — §20. in this book. On page xi, where you find the section on how to use this book, read again Step 2. That's what this diagnostic test is all about.

Test Yourself

THE BASICS

Choose the correct answer by circling the letter. Do not refer to the Answer Key and Explained Answers until after you have answered all 60 questions. Time limit is 60 minutes.

1. In Spanish, the letter *g* in front of the vowels *e* or *i* (as in the Spanish word *general*), is pronounced as the underlined letter in the English word
   A. help   B. jet   C. go   D. argue

2. The double *ll* in a Spanish word, as in *llamo*, is pronounced similarly as in the English word
   A. hello   B. lame   C. yes   D. million

3. The letter *d* in a Spanish word, as in *dar*, is pronounced similarly as in the English word
   A. dare   B. thin   C. dad   D. the

4. In pronouncing a Spanish word, if the word ends in a vowel, *n* or *s,* raise your voice on the vowel in the _____ that last vowel, *n* or *s.*
   A. syllable just in front of
   B. syllable at the beginning of the word
   C. syllable right after
   D. middle of

5. Stressing a vowel means _____ your voice on that vowel.
   A. lowering   B. raising   C. modulating
   D. shouting

6. The punctuation mark called *comillas* is
   A. a comma   B. a period
   C. quotation marks   D. a hyphen

PARTS OF SPEECH

On the line in front of each of the following nouns, write *el* if the noun is masculine or *la* if it is feminine.

7. _____ mano   8. _____ día   9. _____ foto

Write the Spanish words for each of the following.

10. the little girl's doll _____

11. John's book _____

12. little Joseph _____

13. a tall, beautiful, and intelligent woman _____
_____

14. a tall, handsome man _____

15. This sentence is easier than you think. _____

_____

Each of the following sentences contains a blank. From the four choices given, select the one that can be inserted to form a grammatically correct sentence and circle the letter of your choice.

16. ¿La carta? Juan está _____.
    A. la escribiendo
    B. escribiéndola
    C. la escribir
    D. escribirla

17. ¿El libro? José quiere _____.
    A. me lo dar
    B. darmelo
    C. dármelo
    D. démelo

18. Me gustan estos guantes y _____.
    A. esos   B. estas   C. aquello   D. ésos

Read the following paragraph carefully. Then answer the questions under it.

    Antes de regresar a su asiento, Juanita vio a un hombre. Cuando Juanita vio al hombre, ella le dijo: "Buenos días, señor". Juanita le dio al hombre su programa y su pluma para escribir su autógrafo. El hombre lo escribió en el programa que Juanita tenía a la mano.

19. How many Spanish verb forms are there in the preterit tense in the above paragraph?
    A. 5   B. 4   C. 6   D. 3

20. How many Spanish verb forms are there in the imperfect indicative tense in the above paragraph?
    A. 0   B. 1   C. 2   D. 3

21. How many Spanish verb forms are there in the present indicative tense in the above paragraph?
    A. 0   B. 1   C. 2   D. 3

22. Write ten commonly used adverbs in Spanish which do not end in *mente*.
    A. ___   B. ___   C. ___   D. ___   E. ___
    F. ___   G. ___   H. ___   I. ___   J. ___

In the next two questions, read the Spanish statements given and select the best translation into English.

23. Paula trabaja mejor que Anita e Isabel trabaja peor que Elena.
    A. Paula works worse than Anita but Isabel works better than Helen.
    B. Paula travels more than Anita and Isabel travels less than Helen.
    C. Paula works faster than Anita and Isabel works more poorly than Helen.
    D. Paula works better than Anita and Isabel works worse than Helen.

24. María corre tan rápidamente como Enrique.
    A. Mary runs much more rapidly than Henry.
    B. Mary runs as fast as Henry.
    C. Mary runs less rapidly than Henry.
    D. Mary runs faster than Henry.

Each of the following sentences contains a blank. From the four choices given, select the one that can be inserted to form a grammatically correct sentence and circle the letter of your choice.

25. ¿Conoce Ud. ＿＿＿ Roberto?
    A. al   B. a   C. el   D. nothing needed

26. ¿Cuánto dinero me da Ud. ＿＿＿ mi trabajo?
    A. para   B. por   C. para que   D. de

27. Ud. habla español muy bien ＿＿＿ norteamericano.
    A. por un   B. por ser un   C. por ser
    D. para ser

Read the following paragraph carefully. Then answer the question under it.

Yo no puedo ir a la fiesta en casa de Juanita esta noche porque tengo muchas tareas y, como mi madre está enferma, debo quedarme en casa; pero mañana es posible o en tres días.

28. How many conjunctions can you find in the above paragraph?
    A. 5   B. 4   C. 3   D. 2

Complete the following conjunctions by writing on the blank line the Spanish word that is missing.

29. a fin ＿＿＿ que / so that, in order that

30. sin ＿＿＿ / nevertheless, however

SPECIAL
TOPICS

Write the Spanish words for each of the following.

31. What a pretty girl! _____

_____

32. How easy it is! _____

_____

33. What an interesting book! _____

_____

Each of the following sentences contains a blank. From the four choices given, select the one that can be inserted in the blank to form a grammatically correct sentence and circle the letter of your choice.

34. Hacía una hora que yo _____ cuando Ud. entró en la sala de clase.
    A. hablo   B. estoy hablando   C. hablé
    D. hablaba

35. Estaremos en México _____ la semana que viene.
    A. a bordo
    B. a tiempo
    C. a fines de
    D. a través de

36. Para hacer este viaje, tengo que comprar un billete _____ .
    A. de ida y vuelta
    B. de rodillas
    C. de acuerdo
    D. de arriba

37. ¿Cuál es la fecha? — Hoy es el _____ de octubre.
    A. un   B. uno   C. primer   D. primero

38. ¿A cuántos estamos hoy? — Estamos _____ cinco de abril.
    A. el   B. a   C. la   D. al

39. Generalmente, en Nueva York hace frío en _____ .
    A. el verano   B. el invierno   C. la primavera
    D. el otoño

Study the clocks and underneath each clock write on the blank line in Spanish words the time that is given.

40. 41. 42.

_____ _____ _____

Read the statement in English and select the correct equivalent in Spanish by drawing a circle around the letter of your choice.

43. Is there much snow here in winter?
   A. ¿Hay mucha nieve aquí en el verano?
   B. ¿Hay mucha lluvia aquí en la primavera?
   C. ¿Hay mucha nieve aquí en el invierno?
   D. ¿Hay mucho lodo aquí en el invierno?

44. It was snowing when I woke up.
   A. Estaba nevando cuando se despertó.
   B. Estaba nevando cuando me desperté.
   C. Estaba lloviendo cuando me desperté.
   D. Estaba lloviendo cuando se despertó.

45. It was very foggy this morning.
   A. Había mucho polvo esta mañana.
   B. Había neblina esta mañana.
   C. Había mucha neblina esta mañana.
   D. Hay mucha neblina esta mañana.

Each of the following sentences contains a blank. From the four choices given, select the one that can be inserted in the blank to form a sensible and grammatically correct sentence and circle the letter of your choice.

46. Veinte _____ diez son dos.
   A. menos   B. por   C. y   D. dividido por

47. Dos _____ tres son cinco.
   A. menos   B. por   C. y   D. dividido por

48. Cinco _____ seis son treinta.
   A. y   B. por   C. dividido por   D. menos

Read the synonyms in English in each of the following and select the correct equivalent in Spanish by drawing a circle around the letter of your choice.

49. jest, joke, fun
    A. camarero, mozo   B. chiste, chanza, broma
    C. aún, todavía   D. anillo, sortija

50. to break
    A. quebrar, romper   B. esperar, aguardar
    C. burlarse de, mofarse de   D. luchar, pelear

51. to shout, to cry out
    A. cruzar, atravesar   B. rogar, suplicar
    C. dar voces, gritar   D. mostrar, enseñar

Read the words in English that are antonyms in each of the following and select the correct equivalent in Spanish by drawing a circle around the letter of your choice.

52. to have a good time / to be bored
    A. apresurarse a / tardar en
    B. olvidarse de / acordarse de
    C. aparecer / desaparecer
    D. aburrirse / divertirse

53. slowly / quickly
    A. arriba / abajo
    B. aprisa / despacio
    C. barato / caro
    D. flaco / gordo

54. inside / outside
    A. éxito / fracaso
    B. dentro / fuera
    C. hembra / macho
    D. ancho / estrecho

55. Write a word in Spanish that ends in *mente* and is a cognate of a word in English that ends in *ly.*

_____

56. Write a word in Spanish that ends in *ario* and is a cognate of a word in English that ends in *ary.*

_____

57. Write a word in Spanish that ends in *oso* and is a cognate of a word in English that ends in *ous.*

_____

For each Spanish word select the English word whose meaning is the same.

58. éxito
    A. success   B. failure   C. exit   D. exciting

59. constipado
    A. constituted   B. constipated
    C. sick with a common cold   D. farmer

60. vaso
    A. pitcher   B. vase
    C. drinking glass   D. cup

Answers

_____   _____   1. A. Review **§1.**, A Guide to Pronouncing Spanish Sounds, Other Sounds.

_____   _____   2. C. Review **§1.**, where _llave_ is given as an example.

_____   _____   3. D. Review **§1.**, Consonant Sounds, where _dar_ and _this_ are given as examples.

_____   _____   4. A. Review **§2.**

_____   _____   5. B. Review **§2.**

_____   _____   6. C. Review **§2.**

_____   _____   7. _la._ Review **§3.1.**

_____   _____   8. _el._ Review **§3.1.**

_____   _____   9. _la._ Review **§3.1.**

_____   _____   10. _la muñeca de la chiquita._ Review **§4.1 – 1.**

_____   _____   11. _el libro de Juan._ Review **§4.1 – 1.**

_____   _____   12. _el pequeño José._ Review **§4.1 – 1.**

_____   _____   13. _una mujer alta, hermosa e inteligente._ Review **§5.4 – 1.** To understand the use of **y** and **e** (both meaning _and_), consult **§10.2 – 4.**

_____   _____   14. _un hombre alto y hermoso._ Review **§5.4 – 1.**

_____   _____   15. _Esta frase es más fácil de lo que Ud. cree._ Review **§5.6 – 1.**

_____   _____   16. B. Review **§6.1 – 4.**

_____   _____   17. C. Review **§6.1 – 5.**

_____   _____   18. D. Review **§6.3.**

_____   _____   19. A. Review the preterit in **§7.5 – 3.**

_____   _____   20. B. Review the imperfect indicative in **§7.5 – 2.**

_____   _____   21. A. Review the present indicative in **§7.5 – 1.**

_____   _____   22. _abajo, arriba, bien, mal, hoy, mañana, siempre, nunca, aquí, allí._ Review **§8.1.**

_____   _____   23. D. Review irregular comparative adverbs in **§8.2.**

_____   _____   24. B. Review regular comparison of adverbs in **§8.2.**

RIGHT   WRONG
  (check one)

_____   _____   25. B. Review the personal *a* in **§9.5 – 1.**

_____   _____   26. B. Review the uses of *para* and *por* in **§9.5 – 3.**

_____   _____   27. D. Review the uses of *para* and *por* in **§9.5 – 3.**

_____   _____   28. A. Review the common conjunctions in **§10.1.**

_____   _____   29. de. Review the common conjunctions in **§10.1.**

_____   _____   30. embargo. Review the common conjunctions in **§10.1.**

_____   _____   31. *¡Qué chica tan bonita!* Review exclamatory sentences in **§11.**

_____   _____   32. *¡Qué fácil es!* Review exclamatory sentences in **§11.**

_____   _____   33. *¡Qué libro más interesante!* Review exclamatory sentences in **§11.**

_____   _____   34. D. Review the use of *Hacía* + length of time + *que* + imperfect indicative tense in **§12.1.**

_____   _____   35. C. Review common expressions with *a* in **§12.2.**

_____   _____   36. A. Review common expressions with *de,* as in *billete de ida y vuelta* in **§12.2.**

_____   _____   37. D. Review asking and stating the date in **§13.1.**

_____   _____   38. B. Review asking and stating the date in **§13.1.**

_____   _____   39. B. Review the seasons of the year in **§13.4.**

_____   _____   40. *Son las cinco y diez.* Review telling time in **§14.**

_____   _____   41. *Es la una.* Review telling time in **§14.**

_____   _____   42. *Son las seis menos cuarto.* Review telling time in **§14.**

_____   _____   43. C. Review weather expressions in **§15.**

_____   _____   44. B. Review weather expressions in **§15.**

_____   _____   45. C. Review weather expressions in **§15.**

_____   _____   46. D. Review numbers in **§16.** and simple arithmetical expressions in **§16.1.**

_____   _____   47. C. Review numbers in **§16.1.**

_____   _____   48. B. Review numbers in **§16.1.**

_____   _____   49. B. Review synonyms in **§17.**

_____   _____   50. A. Review synonyms in **§17.**

_____   _____   51. C. Review synonyms in **§17.**

RIGHT   WRONG
  (check one)

_____   _____   52. D. Review antonyms in **§18.**

_____   _____   53. B. Review antonyms in **§18.**

_____   _____   54. B. Review antonyms in **§18.**

_____   _____   55. *correctamente, finalmente, naturalmente.* Review cognates in **§19.**

_____   _____   56. *necesario, vocabulario.* Review cognates in **§19.**

_____   _____   57. *famoso, generoso.* Review cognates in **§19.**

_____   _____   58. A. Review tricky words in **§20.**

_____   _____   59. C. Review tricky words in **§20.**

_____   _____   60. C. Review tricky words in **§20.**

Diagnostic Analysis

Section	Question Numbers	Number of Answers	
		Right	Wrong
THE BASICS			
1. Pronunciation	1, 2, 3		
2. Capitalization, Punctuation, Word Division	4, 5, 6		
THE PARTS OF SPEECH			
3. Nouns	7, 8, 9		
4. Articles	10, 11, 12		
5. Adjectives	13, 14, 15		
6. Pronouns	16, 17, 18		
7. Verbs	19, 20, 21		
8. Adverbs	22, 23, 24		
9. Prepositions	25, 26, 27		
10. Conjunctions	28, 29, 30		
SPECIAL TOPICS			
11. Exclamatory Statements	31, 32, 33		
12. Idioms	34, 35, 36		
13. Dates, Days, Months, Seasons	37, 38, 39		
14. Telling Time	40, 41, 42		
15. Weather Expressions	43, 44, 45		
16. Numbers	46, 47, 48		
17. Synonyms	49, 50, 51		
18. Antonyms	52, 53, 54		
19. Cognates	55, 56, 57		
20. Tricky Words	58, 59, 60		
TOTAL QUESTIONS:	60		

Use the following scale to see how you did.

58 to 60 right:	*Excellent*
55 to 57 right:	*Very Good*
52 to 54 right:	*Average*
49 to 51 right:	*Below Average*
Fewer than 49 right:	*Unsatisfactory*

A GRAMMAR BRUSH-UP

In the chapters that follow, a numerical decimal system has been used with the symbol § in front of it. This was done so that you may find quickly and easily the reference to a particular point in Spanish grammar when you use the index. For example, if you look up the entry ''adjectives'' in the index, you will find the reference given as §5. Sometimes additional § reference numbers are given when the entry you consulted is mentioned in other areas in the chapter §. The index also includes some key Spanish words, for example ser and estar, and § references to them are also given.

The Basics

A Guide to Pronouncing Spanish Sounds

English words given here contain sounds that only approximate Spanish sounds.

Phonetic Symbol	Pronounced as in the	
	Spanish Word	**English Word**

PURE VOWEL SOUNDS		
a	*la*	father
e	*le*	ate
i	*ti*	see
o	*yo*	order
u	*tu*	too

DIPHTHONGS (2 vowels together)		
ai	*baile* / *hay*	eye
au	*aula*	cow
ei	*reino* / *ley*	they
eu	*Europa*	wayward
ya	*enviar* / *ya*	yard
ye	*tiene* / *yendo*	yes
yo	*iodo* / *yodo*	yore
yu	*viuda* / *yugo*	you
oy	*oigo* / *estoy*	toy
wa	*cuando*	want
we	*bueno*	way
wi	*suizo*	week
wo	*cuota*	woke

Phonetic Symbol	Pronounced as in the	
	Spanish Word	English Word

TRIPHTHONGS (3 vowels together)

yai	enviáis	yipe
yau	miau	meow
yei	enviéis	yea
wai	guaina	wise
	Uruguay	
wau	guau	wow
wei	continuéis }	wait
	buey	

The accent mark (´) over a vowel sound indicates that you must raise your voice on that vowel sound.

CONSONANT SOUNDS

b	bien	boy
	va	
d	dar	this
f	falda	fan
g	gato	
	goma }	gap
	gusto	
k	casa	
	culpa	
	que }	cap
	quito	
l	la	lard
m	me	may
n	no	no
ɲ	niño	canyon
p	papá	papa
R	pero	April
RR	perro	burr, gr-r-r
s	sopa	
	cero	
	cita }	soft
	zumo	
t	tu	sit
tʃ	mucho	church

OTHER SOUNDS

h	justo	
	general }	help
	gigante	

Phonetic Symbol	Pronounced as in the	
	Spanish Word	**English Word**

OTHER SOUNDS

The letter *h* in a Spanish word is not pronounced.

y	*yo* *llave* }	yes

The pronunciation given in phonetic symbols is that of most Latin American countries and of certain regions in Spain.

§2.

Capitalization, Punctuation Marks, and Division of Words into Syllables

**CAPITALIZA-
TION**

Generally speaking, do not capitalize days of the week, months of the year, languages, nationalities, and religions.

domingo, lunes, martes, etc.; *enero, febrero, marzo,* etc.; *español, francés, inglés,* etc.; *Roberto es español, María es española, Pierre es francés; Elena es católica.*

PUNCTUATION

Common punctuation marks in Spanish are as follows:

apóstrofo / apostrophe '
comillas / quotation marks " "
paréntesis / parentheses ( )
principio de interrogación / beginning question mark ¿
fin de interrogación / final question mark ?
punto / period .
coma / comma ,
punto y coma / semicolon ;
dos puntos / colon :
puntos suspensivos / ellipses . . .

**DIVISION OF
WORDS**

It is good to know how to divide a word into syllables (not only in Spanish but also in English) because it helps you to pronounce the word correctly and to spell it correctly. The general rules to follow when dividing Spanish words into syllables are:

In General

• A syllable must contain a vowel.
• A syllable may contain only one vowel and no consonant: *e / so (eso).*

Consonants

• If you are dealing with single separate consonants, each consonant remains with the vowel that follows it: *mu / cho (mucho), ca / ba / llo (caballo), pe / ro (pero), pe / rro (perro).* Did you notice that the consonants *ch, ll,* and *rr* are considered as one consonant sound and are not separated?
• If you are dealing with two consonants that come together (other than *ch, ll,* or *rr* as stated above), the two consonants are separated; the first remains with the preceding syllable and the second remains with the following syllable when they are split: *her / ma / no (hermano), at / las (atlas), ter / cer (tercer)*

20

But if the second of the two consonants that come together is *l* or *r*, do not separate them: *ha | blo (hablo), a | pren | do (aprendo), li | bro (libro)*
- If you are dealing with three consonants that come together, the first two remain with the preceding vowel and the third consonant remains with the vowel that follows it: *ins | ti | tu | to (instituto)*
But if the third of the three consonants is *l* or *r*, do not separate that third consonant from the second; it remains with the second consonant: *com | pren | der (comprender), sas | tre (sastre), sal | dré (saldré)*

Vowels

- Two vowels that are together are generally separated if they are strong vowels. The strong vowels are: *a, e, o:*
a | e | ro | pla | no (aeroplano), o | a | sis (oasis), re | a | li | dad (realidad)
But if you are dealing with a weak vowel *(i, u)* it ordinarily remains in the same syllable with its neighboring vowel, especially if that other vowel is a strong vowel: *trein | ta (treinta), ru | bio (rubio), hue | vo (huevo)*
- If a vowel contains a written accent mark, it becomes strong enough to remain in its own syllable: *Ma | rí | a (María), re | ú | ne (reúne), dí | a (día)*

Other

- The letter *y* is considered a consonant when a vowel follows it. Keep it with the vowel that follows it: *a | yer (ayer), a | yu | dar (ayudar)*

Syllable Emphasis

If a Spanish word ends in a vowel, the letter *n* or *s*, emphasize the second-to-last syllable of the word:

*mu	CHA	cho*	*re	SU	men*	*mu	CHA	chas*
(boy)	(summary)	(girls)

If a Spanish word ends in a letter other than a vowel, *n* or *s*, emphasize that last syllable:

*com	pren	DER*	*re	a	li	DAD*	*es	pa	ÑOL*
(to understand)	(reality)	(Spanish)

Sometimes, a written accent (´) is placed over the vowel that must be stressed, indicating an exception to the rule. The accent mark tells the reader which vowel to stress:

*LA	piz (lápiz)*	*DE	bil (débil)*
(pencil)	(weak)
*LA	pi	ces (lápices)*	*DE	bi	les (débiles)*
(pencils)	(weak)

Mnemonic tip Most words in Spanish, including verb forms, end in a vowel, *n* or *s*. Therefore, apply the first rule by keeping in mind the following Mnemonic tip:

El muCHAcho y las muCHAchas CANtan en espaÑOL.
(The boy and the girls are singing in Spanish.)

Note, finally, that *el corazón* (heart) requires an accent mark on the vowel *o* because the pronunciation does not follow the simple rule stated above. Spanish-speaking people pronounce the word as *co / ra / ZON* with an accent mark on *ZÓN* to show this exception. There are hundreds of Spanish words that require an accent mark because their pronunciation does not follow the general rule.

The Parts of Speech

§3.

Nouns

DEFINITION

A noun is a word that refers to a person, a place, a thing, or a quality.

Nouns are either masculine or feminine and always require an article: *el, la, los, las.*

The gender of nouns that do not refer to persons or animals, where the gender is apparent, must be learned.

Gender	Noun Endings	Examples
masculine	- o	*el libro*
feminine	- a - ción - sión - dad - tad - tud - umbre	*la casa* *la lección* *la ilusión* *la ciudad* *la dificultad* *la solicitud* *la costumbre*
masculine or feminine, referring to a specific person	- nte	*el estudiante* *la estudiante*
some masculine some feminine	- e	*el aire, el coche* *la gente, la leche*

§3.1 IRREGULAR GENDER OF NOUNS

Ending	Gender	Examples
- o	feminine	*la mano*/hand *la radio* / radio *la foto* / photo
- a	masculine	*el día*/day *el drama* / drama *el clima* / climate
- ista	masculine or feminine, referring to a specific person	*el dentista*⎫ *la dentista*⎭ dentist *el novelista*⎫ *la novelista*⎭ novelist

§3.2 PLURAL OF NOUNS

Noun Ending	Plural	Examples
vowel	add *s*	*el chico* / los chicos
consonant	add *es*	*la flor* / las flores
z	change *z* to *c* and add *es*	*la luz* / las luces

§3.2–1 Other Exceptions

Sometimes a masculine plural noun refers to both male and female persons:

> *los padres* / the parents, the mother and father

Generally, a noun that ends in *ión* drops the accent mark in the plural:

> *la lección* / *las lecciones; la ilusión* / *las ilusiones*

Generally, a noun that ends in *és* drops the accent mark in the plural:

> *el francés* / the Frenchman; *los franceses* / the Frenchmen

Sometimes the accent mark is kept in the plural in order to keep the stress where it is in the singular: *el país* / *los países*

Some nouns have a plural ending but are regarded as singular because they are compound nouns:

> *el paraguas* / the umbrella; *los paraguas* / the umbrellas

Generally speaking, a noun that ends in *s* in the singular with no stress on that final syllable remains the same in the plural: *el lunes* / *los lunes*

Generally speaking, a noun that ends in *s* in the singular with the stress on that syllable requires the addition of *es* to form the plural: *el mes* / *los meses*

Some nouns that contain no accent mark in the singular require an accent mark in the plural:

> *el joven* / the young man; *los jóvenes* / the young men

§3.3 SPECIAL CASES

§3.3 – 1 Nouns Used as Adjectives

It is common in English to use a noun as an adjective: a history class. When this is done in Spanish, the preposition *de* is usually placed in front of the noun that is used as an adjective and both are placed after the noun that is being described:

una clase de historia / a history class (a class of history)
una corbata de seda / a silk tie (a tie of silk)
un reloj de oro / a gold watch (a watch of gold)

Also note that the preposition *para* (for) is used in order to indicate that something is intended for something:

una taza para café / a coffee cup (a cup for coffee)

However, if the cup is filled with coffee, we say in Spanish:

una taza de café / a cup of coffee

§3.3 – 2 Nouns in the Diminutive

Nouns ending in *ito* or *illo*
　Generally speaking, the ending *ito* or *illo* can be added to a noun to form the diminutive form of a noun. This makes the noun take on the meaning of little or small in size:

un vaso / a glass (drinking); *un vasito* / a little drinking glass
una casa / a house; *una casita* / a little house
un cigarro / a cigar; *un cigarillo* / a cigarette

To form the diminutive in Spanish, ordinarily drop the final vowel of the noun and add *ito (ita)* or *illo (illa): una casa / una casita.* If the final letter of the noun is a consonant, merely add *ito* or *illo:*

papel / paper; *papelito* OR *papelillo* / small bit of paper

At other times, these diminutive endings give a favorable quality to the noun, even a term of endearment:

una chica / a girl; *una chiquita* / a cute little girl

Here, note that before dropping the final vowel *a* to add *ita,* you must change *c* to *q* in order to preserve the hard sound of *k* in *chica:*

> *un perro* / a dog; *un perrito* / a darling little dog
> *una abuela* / a grandmother; *abuelita* / "dear old granny"

In English, we do something similar to this:

> drop / droplet; doll / dolly OR dollie; pig / piggy OR piggie OR piglet; bath / bathinette; book / booklet; John / Johnny; Ann / Annie.

§3.3–3
Nouns That Change Meaning According to Gender

Some nouns have one meaning when masculine and another meaning when feminine. Here are two common examples:

Noun	Masculine Gender Meaning	Feminine Gender Meaning
capital	capital (money)	capital (city)
cura	priest	cure

§3.3–4
Campo, País, Patria, Nación

The first three nouns *(el campo, el país, la patria)* all mean country. However, note the following:

- *campo* means country in the sense of countryside:

  > *en el campo* / in the country; *Vamos a pasar el fin de semana en el campo* / We are going to spend the weekend in the country.

- *país* means country in the meaning of nation:

  > *¿En qué país nació Ud.?* / In what country were you born?

- *patria* means country in the sense of native land:

  > *El soldado defendió a su patria.* / The soldier defended his country.

- *nación* means country in the sense of nation:

  > *Las Naciones Unidas* / the United Nations

§3.3 – 5
Hora, Tiempo,
and *Vez*

These three nouns all mean time; however, note the differences:

La hora refers to the time (the hour) of the day:

¿A qué hora vamos al baile? / At what time are we going to the dance? *Vamos al baile a las nueve.* / We are going to the dance at nine o'clock.
¿Qué hora es? / What time is it? *Es la una.* / It is one o'clock.
Son las dos. / It is two o'clock.

El tiempo refers to a vague or indefinite duration of time:

No puedo ir contigo porque no tengo tiempo. / I cannot go with you because I don't have time.

As you know, *tiempo* is also used to express the weather:

¿Qué tiempo hace hoy? / What's the weather like today?
Hace buen tiempo. / The weather is fine.

La vez means time in the sense of occasions or different times:

the first time / *la primera vez;* this time / *esta vez;*
many times / *muchas veces*

§4.

Articles

There are four forms of the definite article (the) in Spanish. They are:

	Singular	Plural
Masculine	*el*	*los*
Feminine	*la*	*las*

EXAMPLES:
el libro (the book) / *los libros* (the books)
la pluma (the pen) / *las plumas* (the pens)

A definite article agrees in gender and number with the noun it modifies.

Noun	Article
m. singular	*el*
m. plural	*los*
f. singular	*la*
f. plural	*las*

If a feminine singular noun begins with stressed *a* or *ha*, use *el*, not *la*. For example, *hambre* (hunger) is a feminine noun but in the singular it is stated as *el hambre*. NOTE: *Tengo mucha hambre.* And NOTE:

el agua / the water; BUT *las aguas* / the waters
el hacha / the axe; BUT *las hachas* / the axes

However, if the definite article is in front of an adjective that precedes the noun, this is not observed:

la alta montaña / the high (tall) mountain
la árida llanura / the arid (dry) prairie

Contraction of the definite article *el*:

When the preposition *a* or *de* is in front of the definite article *el,* it contracts as follows:

> *a + el* changes to *al*
> *de + el* changes to *del*

EXAMPLES:
Voy al parque. / I am going to the park.
Vengo del parque. / I am coming from the park.

But if the definite article *el* is part of a denomination or title of a work, there is no contraction: *Los cuadros de El Greco.*

§4.1–1
The Definite Article Is Used:

• In front of each noun even if there is more than one noun stated, as in a series, which is not always done in English:

   Tengo el libro, el cuaderno, y la pluma. / I have the book, notebook, and pen.

• With a noun when you make a general statement:

   Me gusta el café / I like coffee.

• With a noun of weight or measure:

   un dólar la libra; un peso la libra / one dollar a pound (per pound)

• In front of a noun indicating a profession, rank, title followed by the name of the person:

   El profesor Gómez es inteligente. / Professor Gómez is intelligent.

> But in direct address (when talking directly to the person and you mention the rank, profession, etc.), do not use the definite article:
>
> *Buenas noches, señor Gómez.* / Good evening, Mr. Gómez.

• With the name of a language, it is optional to use the definite article: *Estudio español.* The trend in some Spanish speaking countries is not to use the definite article when the name of the language is the object of a verb.

- With the name of a subject matter:

  Estudio la historia / I study history.

- With the days of the week, when in English we use *on*:

  Voy al cine el sábado / I am going to the movies on Saturday.

- With parts of the body or articles of clothing, especially if the possessor is clearly stated:

  Me pongo el sombrero / I put on my hat.

- With common expressions, for example:

  a la escuela / to school; *en la iglesia* / in church
  la semana pasada / last week

- With the seasons of the year:

  en la primavera / in spring; *en el verano* / in summer;
  en el otoño / in autumn; *en el invierno* / in winter

- To show possession with the preposition *de* + a common noun:

  el libro del alumno / the pupil's book
  los libros de los alumnos / the pupils' books
  la muñeca de la chiquita / the little girl's doll

> Note that when a proper noun is used, the definite article is not needed with *de* to show possession:
>
> *el libro de Juan* / John's book

- With names of some cities, countries and continents: *la Argentina, el Brasil, el Canadá, los Estados Unidos, la Habana, la América del Norte, la América Central, la América del Sur.*

- With a proper noun modified by an adjective:

  el pequeño José / Little Joseph

- With a noun in apposition with a pronoun:

  Nosotros los norteamericanos / We North Americans

- With an infinitive used as a noun, especially when it begins a sentence:

  El estudiar es bueno. / Studying is good.

> There are some exceptions: *Ver es creer* / Seeing is believing; and other proverbs. But you do not normally use the definite article with an infinitive if it does not begin a sentence:
>
> *Es bueno estudiar* / It is good to study.

- When telling time:

  Es la una / It is one o'clock; *Son las dos* / It is two o'clock.

§4.1–2 The Definite Article Is Not Used:

- In direct address with the rank, profession, title of the person to whom you are talking or writing:

  Buenos días, señora Molina. / Good morning, Mrs. Molina.

- After the verb *hablar* when the name of a language is right after a form of *hablar:*

  Hablo español / I speak Spanish.

- After the prepositions *en* and *de* with the name of a language or a subject matter:

  Estoy escribiendo en inglés. / I am writing in English.
  La señora Johnson es profesora de inglés. / Mrs. Johnson is a teacher of English.

- With a proper noun to show possession when using *de:*

  los libros de Marta / Martha's books

- With an infinitive if the infinitive does not begin the sentence:

  Es bueno trabajar. / It is good to work.
  Me gusta viajar. / I like to travel.

- With a noun in apposition with a noun:

  Madrid, capital de España, es una ciudad interesante. / Madrid, capital of Spain, is an interesting city.

- With a numeral that denotes the order of succession of a monarch:

  Carlos V (Quinto) / Charles the Fifth

- With names of some countries and continents:

  España / Spain; *Francia* / France; *México* / Mexico; *Europa* / Europe

§4.2 INDEFINITE ARTICLE

In Spanish, there are four forms of the indefinite article (a, an, some, a few). They are:

	Singular	Plural
Masculine	*un*	*unos*
Feminine	*una*	*unas*

EXAMPLES:
un libro (a book); *unos libros* (some books, a few books)
una naranja (an orange); *unas naranjas* (some oranges, a few oranges)

An indefinite article agrees in gender and number with the noun it modifies.

Noun	Article
m. singular	*un*
m. plural	*unos*
f. singular	*una*
f. plural	*unas*

The plural of the indefinite article indicates an indefinite number:

unas treinta personas / some thirty persons.

§4.2−1 The Indefinite Article Is Used:

• When you want to say a or an. It is also used as a numeral to mean one:

un libro / a book or one book

If you want to make it clear that you mean one, you may use *solamente* (only) in front of *un* or *una:*

Tengo solamente un libro. / I have (only) one book.

• With a modified noun of nationality, profession, rank, or religion:

El doctor Gómez es un médico excelente. / Dr. Gómez is an excellent doctor.

- In front of each noun in a series, which we do not always do in English:

  Tengo un libro, un cuaderno, y una pluma. / I have a book, notebook, and pen.

- In the plural when an indefinite number is indicated:

  Tengo unos dólares. / I have some (a few) dollars.

§4.2 – 2
The Indefinite Article Is Not Used:

- With *cien* and *mil:*

  cien libros / a (one) hundred books
  mil dólares / a (one) thousand dollars

- With *cierto, cierta* and *tal:*

  cierto lugar / a certain place; *cierta persona* / a certain person
  tal hombre / such a man; *tal caso* / such a case

- With *otro, otra:*

  otro libro / another book; *otra pluma* / another pen

- With an unmodified noun of nationality, profession, rank, or religion:

  Mi hijo es dentista. / My son is a dentist.
  Soy mexicano. / I am Mexican.

- When you use *Qué* in an exclamation:

  ¡Qué hombre! / What a man!

- With some negations, particularly with the verb *tener,* or in an interrogative statement before an unmodified noun object:

  ¿Tiene Ud. libro? / Do you have a book?

- With a noun in apposition:

  Martí, gran político y más grande poeta . . . / Martí, a great politician and greatest poet . . .

§4.3
THE NEUTER ARTICLE *LO*

Lo has idiomatic uses, generally speaking.
It is used:

- With a masculine singular form of an adjective used as a noun:

  lo bueno / the good; *lo malo* / the bad
  lo interesante / what(ever) is interesting

- With a past participle:

  lo dicho y lo escrito / what has been said and what has been written

- With an adjective or adverb + *que*, meaning how:

  Veo lo fácil que es. / I see how easy it is.

§5.

Adjectives

DEFINITION

An adjective is a word that describes a noun or pronoun in some way.

§5.1 AGREEMENT

An adjective agrees in gender and number with the noun or pronoun it describes. Gender means masculine, feminine, or neuter. Number means singular or plural.

An adjective that ends in *o* in the masculine singular changes *o* to *a* to form the feminine: *rojo / roja, pequeño / pequeña.*

An adjective that expresses a person's nationality, which ends in a consonant, requires the addition of *a* to form the feminine singular:

Juan es español / María es española.

An adjective that ends in *e* generally does not change to form the feminine: *un muchacho inteligente / una muchacha inteligente.*

An adjective that ends in a consonant generally does not change to form the feminine: *una pregunta difícil / un libro difícil*—except for an adjective of nationality, as stated above, and adjectives that end in *-án, -ón, -ín, -or* (*trabajador / trabajadora,* industrious).

§5.2 POSITION

Normally, a descriptive adjective is placed after the noun it describes: *una casa amarilla.*

Two descriptive adjectives, *bueno* and *malo,* are sometimes placed in front of the noun. When placed in front of a masculine singular noun, the *o* drops: *un buen amigo; un mal alumno.*

A limiting adjective is generally placed in front of the noun: *algunos estudiantes; mucho dinero.*

In an interrogative sentence, the predicate adjective precedes the subject when it is a noun: *¿Es bonita María?*

Some adjectives have a different meaning depending on their position.

un nuevo sombrero / a new (different, another) hat *un sombrero nuevo* / a new (brand new) hat
un gran hombre / a great man *un hombre grande* / a large, big man
una gran mujer / a great woman *una mujer grande* / a large, big woman
la pobre niña / the poor girl (unfortunate, unlucky) *la niña pobre* / the poor girl (poor, not rich)

§5.3 PLURAL OF ADJECTIVES

Like nouns, to form the plural of an adjective, add *s* if the adjective ends in a vowel: *blanco / blancos; blanca / blancas*.

If an adjective ends in a consonant, add *es* to form the plural: *español / españoles; difícil / difíciles*.

> Note that the accent on *difícil* remains in the plural in order to keep the stress there: *difíciles*.

Some adjectives drop the accent mark in the plural because it is not needed to indicate the stress. The stress falls naturally on the same vowel in the plural: *cortés / corteses; alemán / alemanes*.

Some adjectives add the accent mark in the plural because the stress needs to be kept on the vowel that was stressed in the singular where no accent mark was needed. In the singular, the stress falls naturally on that vowel: *joven / jóvenes*.

An adjective that ends in *z* changes *z* to *c* and adds *es* to form the plural: *feliz / felices*.

If an adjective describes or modifies two or more nouns that are all masculine, naturally the masculine plural is used: *Roberto y Felipe están cansados*.

If an adjective describes or modifies two or more nouns that are all feminine, naturally the feminine plural is used: *Elena y Marta están cansadas*.

If an adjective describes or modifies two or more nouns of different genders, the masculine plural is used: *María, Elena, Marta, y Roberto están cansados*.

§5.4
TYPES

§5.4-1
Descriptive
Adjectives

A descriptive adjective is a word that describes a noun or pronoun: *casa blanca, chicas bonitas, chicos altos; Ella es bonita.*

Two or more descriptive adjectives of equal importance are placed after the noun. If there are two, they are joined by *y* (or *e*). If there are more than two, the last two are connected by *y* (or *e*):

un hombre alto y hermoso / a tall, handsome man
una mujer alta, hermosa e inteligente / a tall, beautiful and
intelligent woman

§5.4-2
Limiting
Adjectives

A limiting adjective limits the number of the noun: *una casa, un libro, algunos muchachos, muchas veces.*

§5.4-3
Demonstrative
Adjectives

A demonstrative adjective is used to point out someone or something. Like other adjectives, a demonstrative adjective agrees in gender and number with the noun it modifies. The demonstrative adjectives are:

English Meaning	Masculine	Feminine
this (here)	*este libro*	*esta pluma*
these (here)	*estos libros*	*estas plumas*
that (there)	*ese libro*	*esa pluma*
those (there)	*esos libros*	*esas plumas*
that (farther away or out of sight)	*aquel libro*	*aquella pluma*
those (farther away or out of sight)	*aquellos libros*	*aquellas plumas*

If there is more than one noun, a demonstrative adjective is ordinarily used in front of each noun:

este hombre y esta mujer / this man and (this) woman

The demonstrative adjectives are used to form the demonstrative pronouns.

| Mnemonic tip | To distinguish between *este libro* (this book) and *ese libro* (that book), remember that the *t* in *este libro* (this book near me) falls off on its way to *ese libro* (that book near you). |

§5.4–4 Possessive Adjectives

A possessive adjective is a word that shows possession and it agrees in gender and number with the noun, not with the possessor. A short form of a possessive adjective is placed in front of the noun. If there is more than one noun stated, a possessive adjective is needed in front of each noun:

mi madre y mi padre / my mother and (my) father

There are two forms for the possessive adjectives: the short form and the long form. The short form is placed in front of the noun. The short forms are:

English Meaning	Before a Singular Noun	Before a Plural Noun
1. my	*mi amigo, mi amiga*	*mis amigos, mis amigas*
2. your	*tu amigo, tu amiga*	*tus amigos, tus amigas*
3. your, his, her, its	*su amigo, su amiga*	*sus amigos, sus amigas*
1. our	*nuestro amigo*	*nuestros amigos*
	nuestra amiga	*nuestras amigas*
2. your	*vuestro amigo*	*vuestros amigos*
	vuestra amiga	*vuestras amigas*
3. your, their	*su amigo, su amiga*	*sus amigos, sus amigas*

In order to clarify the meanings of *su* or *sus,* when there might be ambiguity, do the following: Replace *su* or *sus* with the definite article + the noun and add *de Ud., de él, de ella, de Uds., de ellos, de ellas:*

su libro OR *el libro de Ud., el libro de él, el libro de ella; el libro de Uds., el libro de ellos, el libro de ellas*
sus libros OR *los libros de Ud., los libros de él, los libros de ella; los libros de Uds., los libros de ellos, los libros de ellas*

The long form is placed after the noun. The long forms are:

English Meaning	After a Singular Noun	After a Plural Noun
1. my; (of) mine	*mío, mía*	*míos, mías*
2. your; (of) yours	*tuyo, tuya*	*tuyos, tuyas*
3. your, his, her, its; (of yours, of his, of hers, of its)	*suyo, suya*	*suyos, suyas*
1. our; (of) ours	*nuestro, nuestra*	*nuestros, nuestras*
2. your; (of) yours	*vuestro, vuestra*	*vuestros, vuestras*
3. your, their; (of yours, of theirs)	*suyo, suya*	*suyos, suyas*

EXAMPLES:

amigo mío / my friend; *un amigo mío* / a friend of mine

The long forms are used primarily:

- When you are talking directly to someone or when writing a letter to someone:

  ¡Hola, amigo mío! ¿Qué tal? / Hello, my friend! How are things?

- When you want to express "of mine," "of yours," "of his," "of hers," etc.
- With the verb *ser*: *Estos libros son míos* / These books are mine.
- In the expression: *¡Dios mío!* / My heavens! My God!

In order to clarify the meanings of *suyo, suya, suyos, suyas* (since they are third person singular or plural), do the same as for *su* and *sus* above: *dos amigos suyos* can be clarified as: *dos amigos de Ud., dos amigos de él,* (two friends of yours, of his).

The long forms of the possessive adjectives are used to serve as possessive pronouns.

A possessive adjective is ordinarily not used when referring to an article of clothing being worn or to parts of the body, particularly when a reflexive verb is used:

Me lavo las manos antes de comer / I wash my hands before eating.

§5.4–5
Interrogatives

¿Qué . . . ? and *¿cuál . . . ?*

- These two interrogative words both mean "what" or "which" but there is a difference in use:
- Use *¿Qué . . . ?* as a pronoun (when there is no noun right after it) if you are inquiring about something, if you want an explanation about something, if you want something defined or described:

  ¿Qué es esto? / What is this?

- Use *¿Qué . . . ?* as an adjective, when there is a noun right after it:

  ¿Qué día es hoy? / What day is it today?

- Use *¿Cuál . . . ?* as a pronoun, when there is no noun right after it. If by "what" you mean "which" or, "which one," it is better Spanish to use *¿Cuál . . . ?* For example:

  ¿Cuál de estos lápices es mejor? / Which (Which one) of these pencils is better?

- The same is true in the plural:

  ¿Cuáles son buenos? / Which ones are good?

- Do not use *cuál* if there is a noun right after it; in that case, you must use *qué,* as noted above.

§5.4–6
As Nouns

At times, an adjective is used as a noun if it is preceded by an article or a demonstrative adjective:

el viejo / the old man; *aquel viejo* / that old man;
la joven / the young lady; *estos jóvenes* / these young men;
este ciego / this blind man

§5.5
SHORTENED
FORMS

Certain masculine singular adjectives drop the final *o* when in front of a masculine singular noun:

alguno: algún día	*primero: el primer año*
bueno: un buen amigo	*tercero: el tercer mes*
malo: mal tiempo	*uno: un dólar*
ninguno: ningún libro	

Note that when *alguno* and *ninguno* are shortened, an accent mark is required on the *u*.

Santo shortens to *San* before a masculine singular saint: *San Francisco, San José* but remains *Santo* in front of *Do-* or *To-*: *Santo Domingo, Santo Tomás*.

Grande shortens to *gran* when in front of any singular noun, whether masculine or feminine:

un gran hombre / a great (famous) man

Ciento shortens to *cien* when in front of any plural noun, whether masculine or feminine:

cien libros / one (a) hundred books
cien sillas / one (a) hundred chairs

Ciento shortens to *cien* except in the numbers 101 through 199:

cien mil / one hundred thousand
ciento tres dólares / one hundred three dollars

Note that in English we say one hundred or a hundred, but in Spanish no word is used in front of *ciento* or *cien* to express one or a; it is merely *ciento* or *cien*.

Cualquiera and *cualesquiera* lose the final *a* in front of a noun: *cualquier hombre*.

§5.6
COMPARATIVES
AND
SUPERLATIVES

§5.6–1
Comparatives

Of equality: *tan . . . como* (as . . . as)   *María es tan alta como Elena* / Mary is as tall as Helen.
Of a lesser degree: *menos . . . que* (less . . . than)   *María es menos alta que Anita.* / Mary is less tall than Anita.
Of a higher degree: *más . . . que* (more . . . than)   *María es más alta que Isabel.* / Mary is taller than Elizabeth.

COMPARISON BETWEEN TWO CLAUSES

* Use *de lo que* to express "than" when comparing two clauses with different verbs if an adjective or adverb is the comparison:

Esta frase es más fácil de lo que Ud. cree / This sentence is easier than you think.

- Use the appropriate form of *de lo que, de los que, de la que, de las que* when comparing two clauses with the same verbs if a noun is the comparison:

  Tengo más dinero de lo que Ud. tiene / I have more money than you have.
  Roberto tiene más amigas de las que tiene Juan / Robert has more girl friends than John has.

§5.6 – 2
Superlatives

To express the superlative degree, use the comparative forms given above with the appropriate definite article:

With a proper noun. *Anita es la más alta* / Anita is the tallest.
Anita y Roberto son los más altos / Anita and Robert are the tallest.
With a common noun. *El muchacho más alto de la clase es Roberto* / The tallest boy in the class is Robert.

> Note that after a superlative in Spanish, ''in'' is expressed by *de,* not *en.*

When two or more superlative adjectives describe the same noun, *más* or *menos* is used only once in front of the first adjective: *Aquella mujer es la más pobre y vieja.*

Absolute superlative: adjectives ending in *-ísimo, -ísima, -ísimos, -ísimas*

To express an adjective in a very high degree, drop the final vowel (if there is one) and add the appropriate ending among the following, depending on the correct agreement: *-ísimo, -ísima, -ísimos, -ísimas:*

María está contentísima. / Mary is very (extremely) happy.
Los muchachos están contentísimos.

These forms may be used instead of *muy* + adjective:

una casa grandísima / una casa muy grande

Never use *muy* in front of *mucho.* Say *muchísimo.*

Muchísimas gracias. / many thanks; thank you very, very much.

§5.6–3 Irregular Comparatives and Superlatives

Adjective	Comparative	Superlative
bueno (good)	mejor (better)	el mejor (best)
malo (bad)	peor (worse)	el peor (worst)
grande (large)	más grande (larger) mayor (greater, older)	el más grande (largest) el mayor (greatest, oldest)
pequeño (small)	más pequeño (smaller) menor (smaller, younger)	el más pequeño (smallest) el menor (smallest, youngest)

Note that you must be careful to make the correct agreement in gender and number.

- *Más que* (more than) or *menos que* (less than) becomes *más de, menos de* + a number:

  El Señor Gómez tiene más de cincuenta años.
  BUT: *No tengo más que dos dólares.* / I have only two dollars.

In this example, the meaning is "only," expressed by *no* in front of the verb; in this case, you must keep *que* to express "only."

- *Tanto, tanta, tantos, tantas* + noun + *como:* as much (as many) . . . as

  Tengo tanto dinero como usted. / I have as much money as you.
  Tengo tantos libros como usted. / I have as many books as you.

- *Cuanto más (menos)* . . . *tanto más (menos).* / the more (the less) . . . the more (less)
  A proportion or ratio is expressed by this phrase.

  Cuanto más dinero tengo, tanto más necesito. / The more money I have, the more I need.
  Cuanto menos dinero tengo, tanto menos necesito. / The less money I have, the less I need.

A note about the adjectives poco and pequeño:

These two adjectives mean "little," but note the difference.
Poco means "little" in terms of quantity:

Tenemos poco trabajo hoy. / We have little work today.

Pequeño means "little" in terms of size:

Mi casa es pequeña. / My house is small.

§6.

Pronouns

DEFINITION

A pronoun is a word that takes the place of a noun; for example, in English there are these common pronouns: I, you, he, she, it, we, they, me, him, her, us, them—just to mention a few.

TYPES

Pronouns are divided into certain types: personal, prepositional, demonstrative, possessive, relative, interrogative, indefinite and negative.

**§6.1
Personal
Pronouns**

A personal pronoun is used as the subject of a verb, direct or indirect object of a verb, as a reflexive pronoun object, and as object of a preposition.

§6.1–1 Subject Pronouns

Singular	Examples
yo / I	*Yo hablo.*
tú / you (familiar)	*Tú hablas.*
usted / you (polite)	*Usted habla.*
él / he, it	*Él habla.*
ella / she, it	*Ella habla.*
Plural	Examples
nosotros (nosotras) / we	*Nosotros hablamos.*
vosotros (vosotras) / you (fam.)	*Vosotros habláis.*
ustedes / you (polite)	*Ustedes hablan.*
ellos / they	*Ellos hablan.*
ellas / they	*Ellas hablan.*

In Spanish, subject pronouns are not used at all times. The ending of the verb tells you if the subject is 1st, 2nd, or 3rd person in the singular or plural. Of course, in the 3rd person singular and plural there is more than one possible subject with the same ending on the verb form. In that case, if there is any doubt as to what the subject is, it is mentioned for the sake of clarity. At other times, subject pronouns in Spanish are used when you want to be emphatic, to make a contrast between this person and that person, or out of simple courtesy.

§6.1 – 2 Direct Object Pronouns

Singular	Examples
me / me	*María me ha visto.* / Mary has seen me.
te / you (fam.)	*María te había visto.* / Mary had seen you.
le, la / you	*María le (la) ve.* / Mary sees you.
le / him; *lo* / him, it	*María le (lo) ve.* / Mary sees him (it).
la / her, it	*María la ve.* / Mary sees her (it).
Plural	Examples
nos / us	*María nos había visto.* / Mary had seen us.
os / you (fam.)	*María os ha visto.* / Mary has seen you.
los, las / you	*María los (las) ve.* / Mary sees you.
los / them	*María los ve.* / Mary sees them.
las / them	*María las ve.* / Mary sees them.

In Latin American countries, *lo* is generally used instead of *le* to mean "him." The plural of *le* as direct object pronoun is *los.*

Note that in the 3rd person plural, the direct objects *los* (m) and *las* (f) refer to people and things.

Also note that in the 3rd person singular, the direct object pronoun *le* is masculine and *la* is feminine and both mean "you."

3d PERSON DIRECT OBJECT PRONOUNS		
Spanish	**English**	**Gender**
le	him, you	m
lo	him, it	m
la	her, you, it	f
los	you (pl.), them	m
las	you (pl.), them	f

There is also the neuter *lo* direct object pronoun. It usually refers to an idea or a statement:

¿Está Ud. enfermo? / Are you sick? *Sí, lo estoy* / Yes, I am.
¿Son amigos? / Are they friends? *Sí, lo son* / Yes, they are.

Of course, your reply could be *Sí, estoy enfermo* and *Sí, son amigos.* But because your verb is a form of *estar* or *ser,* you do not have to repeat what was mentioned; neuter *lo* takes its place as a direct object pronoun. This neuter *lo* direct object pronoun is also used with other verbs, e.g., *pedir, preguntar* and *parecer:*

> *María parece contenta* / Mary seems happy.
> *Sí, lo parece* / Yes, she does (Yes, she does seem so).

To make the examples in Spanish given above negative, place *no* in front of the direct object pronouns: *María no me ve.* To make the examples in §6.1–1 negative, place *no* in front of the verb.

§6.1–3 Indirect Object Pronouns

Singular	Examples
me / to me	*Pablo me ha hablado* / Paul has talked to me.
te / to you (fam.)	*Pablo te habla* / Paul talks to you.
le / to you, to him, to her, to it	*Pablo le habla* / Paul talks to you (to him, to her, to it).
Plural	Examples
nos / to us	*Pablo nos ha hablado* / Paul has talked to us.
os / to you (fam.)	*Pablo os habla* / Paul talks to you.
les / to you, to them	*Pablo les habla* / Paul talks to you (to them).

To make these sentences negative, place *no* in front of the indirect object pronouns:

> *Pablo no me habla* / Paul does not talk to me.

Note that *me, te, nos, os* are direct object pronouns and indirect object pronouns.

> Note that *le* as an indirect object pronoun has more than one meaning. If there is any doubt as to the meaning, merely add after the verb any of the following accordingly to clarify the meaning:
>
> > *a Ud., a él, a ella: Pablo le habla a usted* / Paul is talking to you.

> Note that *les* has more than one meaning. If there is any doubt as to the meaning, merely add after the verb any of the following, accordingly:
>
> *a Uds., a ellos, a ellas: Pablo no les habla a ellos* / Paul is not talking to them.

As you can see in the examples given above, an indirect object pronoun ordinarily is placed in front of the main verb. Other positions are discussed later in this chapter.

An indirect object pronoun is needed when you use a verb that indicates a person is being deprived of something, e.g., to steal something from someone, to take something off or from someone, to buy something from someone, and actions of this sort. The reason an indirect object pronoun is needed is that you are dealing with the preposition *a* + noun or pronoun and it must be accounted for.

Los ladrones le robaron todo el dinero a él / The robbers stole all the money from him.

La madre le quitó al niño el sombrero / The mother took off the child's hat.

The indirect object pronouns are used with the verb *gustar* and with the following verbs: *bastar, faltar* or *hacer falta, quedarle (a uno), tocarle (a uno), placer, parecer.*

A Ricardo le gusta el helado / Richard likes ice cream (i.e., Ice cream is pleasing to him, to Richard).

A Juan le bastan cien dólares / One hundred dollars are enough for John.

A los muchachos les faltan cinco dólares / The boys need five dollars (i.e., Five dollars are lacking to them, to the boys).

OR

A la mujer le hacen falta cinco dólares / The woman needs five dollars (i.e., Five dollars are lacking to her, to the woman).

§6.1 – 4 Position of Object Pronouns

Let's review the normal position of a single object pronoun when dealing with a simple tense or a compound tense.

Attach the single object pronoun to an infinitive:

Juan quiere escribirlo. / John wants to write it.

If the main verb is *poder, querer, saber, ir a,* you may place the object pronoun in front of the main verb:

Juan lo quiere escribir. / John wants to write it.
¿Puedo levantarme? OR *¿Me puedo levantar?* / May I get up?

Attach the single object pronoun to a present participle:

Juan está escribiéndolo. / John is writing it.

Note that when you attach an object pronoun to a present participle, you must add an accent mark on the vowel that was stressed in the present participle before the object pronoun was attached.

If the main verb is a progressive form with *estar* or another auxiliary, you may place the object pronoun in front of the main verb:

Juan lo está escribiendo. / John is writing it.

When you are dealing with a verb form in the affirmative imperative (command), you must attach the single object pronoun to the verb form and add an accent mark on the vowel that was stressed in the verb form before the single object pronoun was added.

¡Hábleme Ud., por favor! / Talk to me, please!

When you are dealing with a verb form in the negative imperative (command), you must place the object pronoun in front of the verb form.

¡No me hable Ud., por favor! / Do not talk to me, please!

§6.1–5 Position of Double Object Pronouns: A Summary

An indirect object pronoun is always placed in front of a direct object pronoun.

> With a verb in a simple tense or in a compound tense in the affirmative or negative:
> The indirect object pronoun is placed in front of the direct object pronoun and both are placed in front of the verb form.
>
> *Juan me lo da* / John is giving it to me.
> *Juan nos los dio* / John gave them to us.
> *María no me lo ha dado* / Mary has not given it to me.

With a verb in a simple tense or in a compound tense in the interrogative:

The indirect object pronoun remains in front of the direct object pronoun and both remain in front of the verb form. The subject (whether a noun or pronoun) is placed after the verb form.

¿Nos la dio Juan? / Did John give it to us?

With a verb in the affirmative imperative (command):

The object pronouns are still in the same order (indirect object + direct object) but they are attached to the verb form and an accent mark is added on the vowel that was stressed in the verb form before the two object pronouns were added.

¡Dígamelo Ud., por favor! / Tell it to me, please!

With a verb in the negative imperative (command):

The position of *no* and the two object pronouns is the same as usual, in front of the verb form.

¡No me lo diga Ud., por favor! / Don't tell it to me, please!

When dealing with an infinitive, attach both object pronouns (indirect, direct) to the infinitive.

Juan quiere dármelo / John wants to give it to me.

OR

If the main verb is *poder, querer, saber, ir a,* you may place the two object pronouns in front of the main verb.

Juan me lo quiere dar / John wants to give it to me.

When dealing with a present participle, attach both object pronouns (indirect, direct) to the present participle:

Juan está escribiéndomelo / John is writing it to me.

OR

If the main verb is a progressive form with *estar* or another auxiliary, you may place the two object pronouns (indirect, direct) in front of the main verb:

Juan me lo está escribiendo / John is writing it to me.
Juana me lo estaba escribiendo / Jane was writing it to me.

When an indirect object pronoun and a direct object pronoun are both 3rd person, the indirect object pronoun (*le* or *les*) changes to *se* because it cannot stand as *le* or *les* in front of a direct object pronoun beginning with the letter "l."

Juan se lo da / John is giving it to you (to him, to her, to it, to you [plural], to them).
¡Dígaselo Ud.! / Tell it to him!
¡No se lo diga Ud.! / Don't tell it to him!
Juan quiere dárselo.
Juan se lo quiere dar.} John wants to give it to her.
Juan está escribiéndoselo.
Juan se lo está escribiendo.} John is writing it to them.

Since the form *se* can have more than one meaning (to him, to her, to them, etc.), in addition to the fact that it looks exactly like the reflexive pronoun *se,* any doubt as to its meaning can be clarified merely by adding any of the following accordingly: *a Ud., a él, a ella, a Uds., a ellos, a ellas.*

Mnemonic tip   When you are dealing with double object pronouns (one direct and the other indirect), remember that people are more important than things; therefore, the indirect object pronoun (usually referring to a person) goes in front of the direct object pronoun (usually referring to a thing).

§6.1 – 6 Reflexive Pronouns

Singular	Examples
me / myself	Me lavo / I wash myself.
te / yourself	Te lavas / You wash yourself.
se / yourself, himself, herself, itself	Ud. se lava / You wash yourself; Pablo se lava / Paul washes himself, etc.
Plural	**Examples**
nos / ourselves	Nosotros (-as) nos lavamos.
os / yourselves	Vosotros (-as) os laváis.
se / yourselves, themselves	Uds. se lavan / You wash yourselves; Ellos (Ellas) se lavan / They wash themselves.

A reflexive verb contains a reflexive pronoun, and the action of the verb falls on the subject and its reflexive pronoun either directly or indirectly. For that reason the reflexive pronoun must agree with the subject: *yo me . . . , tú te . . . , Ud. se . . . , él se . . . , ella se . . . , nosotros nos . . . , vosotros os . . . , Uds. se . . . , ellos se . . . , ellas se . . . .*

A reflexive pronoun is ordinarily placed in front of the verb form, as you can see in the examples given above.

To make these sentences negative, place *no* in front of the reflexive pronoun: *Yo no me lavo, Tú no te lavas, Ud. no se lava,* etc.

Note that *me, te, nos, os* are not only reflexive pronouns but they are also direct object pronouns and indirect object pronouns.

A reflexive verb in Spanish is not always reflexive in English.

Spanish	English
levantarse	to get up
sentarse	to sit down

There are some reflexive verbs in Spanish that are also reflexive in English.

Spanish	English
bañarse	to bathe oneself
lavarse	to wash oneself

The following reflexive pronouns are also used as reciprocal pronouns, meaning "each other" or "to each other": *se, nos, os.*

Ayer por la noche, María y yo nos vimos en el cine / Yesterday evening, Mary and I saw each other at the movies.
Roberto y Teresa se escriben todos los días / Robert and Teresa write to each other every day.

If the meaning of these three reflexive pronouns is not clear when they are used in a reciprocal meaning, any of the following may be added accordingly to express the idea of "each other" or "to each other": *uno a otro, una a otra, unos a otros,* etc.

If you are dealing with a reflexive pronoun, it is normally placed in front of an object pronoun.

Yo me lo puse / I put it on (me, on myself).

§6.2 Prepositional Pronouns

Pronouns that are used as objects of prepositions are called prepositional pronouns or disjunctive pronouns. They are:

Singular	Plural
para mí / for me, for myself	*para nosotros (nosotras)* / for us, for ourselves
para ti / for you, for yourself	*para vosotros (vosotras)* / for you, for yourselves
para usted (Ud.) / for you	*para ustedes (Uds.)* / for you
para él / for him, for it	*para ellos* / for them
para ella / for her, for it	*para ellas* / for them

Note the following exceptions with the prepositions *con, entre,* and *menos:*

conmigo / with me
contigo / with you (fam.)
consigo / with yourself, with yourselves, with himself, with herself, with themselves

entre tú y yo / between you and me
menos yo / except me

§6.3
Demonstrative
Pronouns

Demonstrative pronouns are formed from the demonstrative adjectives. To form a demonstrative pronoun write an accent mark on the stressed vowel of a demonstrative adjective. A demonstrative pronoun takes the place of a noun. It agrees in gender and number with the noun it replaces. The demonstrative pronouns are:

Masculine	Feminine	Neuter	English Meaning
éste	*ésta*	*esto*	this one (here)
éstos	*éstas*		these (here)
ése	*ésa*	*eso*	that one (there)
ésos	*ésas*		those (there)
aquél	*aquélla*	*aquello*	that one ⎧ (farther
aquéllos	*aquéllas*		those ⎨ away or
			⎩ out of sight)

EXAMPLES:

Me gustan este cuadro y ése / I like this picture and that one.
Estas camisas y aquéllas son hermosas / These shirts and
    those are beautiful.

| Mnemonic tip | To help you remember that a demonstrative pronoun is formed from a demonstrative adjective, regard the written accent mark (´) over the stressed vowel in the demonstrative pronoun as a marker that makes the word stand alone as a pronoun. As such, there is no noun after it; but there is a noun after the demonstrative adjective: *este libro* / this book; *éste* / this one.

§6.3 – 1 Neuter Forms

Note that the neuter forms do not have an accent mark. They are not used when you are referring to a particular noun. They are used when referring to an idea, a statement, a situation, a clause, a phrase. Never use the neuter pronouns to refer to a person.

¿Qué es esto? / What is this?
Eso es fácil de hacer / That is easy to do.
Juan no estudia y esto me inquieta / John does not study and
                this worries me.

Note also that the English term "the latter" is expressed in Spanish as *éste, ésta, éstos,* or *éstas;* and "the former" is expressed in Spanish as *aquél, aquélla, aquéllos, aquéllas* —depending on the gender and number of the noun referred to.

The pronouns *el de, la de, los de, las de; el que, la que, los que, las que* are used in place of nouns.

EXAMPLES:

> *mi hermano y el (hermano) de mi amigo* / my brother and my friend's
> *mi hermana y la (hermana) de mi amigo* / my sister and my friend's
> *mis hermanos y los (hermanos) del muchacho* / my brothers and the boy's
> *El (muchacho) que baila con María es mi hermano* /The one (boy) who is dancing with Mary is my brother.
> *La (muchacha) que baila con Roberto es mi hermana* /The one (girl) who is dancing with Robert is my sister.
> *Las (muchachas) que bailan son mis amigas* / The ones (girls) who are dancing are my friends.

§6.4 Possessive Pronouns

A possessive pronoun is a word that takes the place of a noun to show possession, as in English: mine, yours, etc.

You form a possessive pronoun by using the appropriate definite article *(el, la, los, las)* + the long form of the possessive adjective. A possessive pronoun agrees in gender and number with the noun it replaces. It does not agree with the possessor.

The possessive pronouns are:

English Meaning	Singular Form (agrees in gender and number with the noun it replaces)	Plural Form (agrees in gender and number with the noun it replaces)
mine	*el mío, la mía*	*los míos, las mías*
yours (fam. sing.)	*el tuyo, la tuya*	*los tuyos, las tuyas*
yours, his, hers, its	*el suyo, la suya*	*los suyos, las suyas*
ours	*el nuestro, la nuestra*	*los nuestros, las nuestras*
yours (fam. pl.)	*el vuestro, la vuestra*	*los vuestros, las vuestras*
yours, theirs	*el suyo, la suya*	*los suyos, las suyas*

EXAMPLES:

Mi hermano es más alto que el suyo / My brother is taller than
yours (his, hers, theirs).
Su hermana es más alta que la mía / Your sister is taller than mine.

In order to clarify the meanings of *el suyo, la suya, los suyos, las suyas* (since they can mean yours, his, hers, its, theirs), drop the *suyo* form, keep the appropriate definite article *(el, la, los, las)*, and add any of the following: *de Ud., de él, de ella, de Uds., de ellos, de ellas.*

mi libro y el de Ud., mi casa y la de él, mis amigos y los de ella, mis amigas y las de Uds. / my book and yours, my house and his, my friends and hers, my friends and yours, etc.

§6.4 – 1 *¿De quién es . . . ? ¿De quiénes es . . . ?* / Whose is . . . ? *¿De quién son . . . ? ¿De quiénes son . . . ?* / Whose are . . . ?

"Whose," when asking a question (usually at the beginning of a sentence), is expressed by any of the above. If you believe that the possessor is singular, use *¿De quién es . . . ?* If you think that the possessor is plural, use *¿De quiénes es . . . ?* And if the noun you have in mind (whose . . .) is plural, use the third person plural form of *ser:*

¿De quién es esta casa? / Whose is this house?
Es de mi tío / It is my uncle's.
¿De quiénes es esta casa? / Whose is this house?
Es de mis amigos / It is my friends'.
¿De quién son estos guantes? / Whose are these gloves?
Son de Juan / They are John's.
¿De quiénes son estos niños? / Whose are these children?
Son de los Señores Pardo / They are Mr. and Mrs. Pardo's.

Note that the verb *ser* is used in these expressions showing possession.

Also note that if a possessive pronoun is used with the verb *ser,* the definite article is dropped:

¿De quién es este lápiz? / Whose is this pencil?
Es mío / It is mine.
¿De quién son estas camisas? / Whose are these shirts?
Son suyas / They are theirs (yours, his, hers).

OR,

Son de Ud., Son de él, Son de ella / They are yours, They are his, They are hers.

§6.5 Relative Pronouns

A pronoun is a word that takes the place of a noun. A relative pronoun is a pronoun that refers to an antecedent. An antecedent is something that comes before something; it can be a word, a phrase, or a clause that is replaced by a pronoun or some other substitute. Example: "Is it Mary who did that?" In this sentence, "who" is the relative pronoun and "Mary" is the antecedent.

In Spanish, a relative pronoun can refer to an antecedent that is a person or a thing, or an idea. A relative pronoun can be subject or object of a verb, or object of a preposition.

§6.5 – 1 *que* / who, that, whom, which

- As subject referring to a person:

  La muchacha que habla con Juan es mi hermana / The girl who is talking with John is my sister.

  The relative pronoun *que* is subject of the verb *habla* and refers to *la muchacha,* which is the subject of *es.*

- As subject referring to a thing:

  El libro que está en la mesa es mío / The book which (that) is on the table is mine.

  The relative pronoun *que* is subject of the verb *está* and refers to *el libro,* which is the subject of *es.*

- As direct object of a verb referring to a person:

  El señor Molina es el profesor que admiro / Mr. Molina is the professor whom I admire.

  The relative pronoun *que* is object of the verb form *admiro.* It refers to *el profesor.*

- As direct object of a verb referring to a thing:

  La composición que Ud. lee es mía / The composition (that, which) you are reading is mine.

  Note in the English translation of this example, that we do not always use a relative pronoun in English. In Spanish, it must be stated.

- As object of a preposition referring only to a thing:

  La cama en que duermo es grande / The bed in which I sleep is large.

The relative pronoun *que* is object of the preposition *en*. It refers to *la cama*. Other prepositions used commonly with *que* are *a, con, de.*

• As object of a preposition, *que* refers to a thing only—not to a person. Use *quien* or *quienes* as object of a preposition referring to persons.

§6.5–2 *quien* / who

• As subject of a verb referring only to persons:

Yo sé quien lo hizo / I know who did it.

Quien is the subject of *hizo*. It does not refer to a specific antecedent. Here, *quien* includes its antecedent.

When used as a subject, *quien* (or *quienes,* if plural) can also mean he who, she who, the one who, the ones who, those who. In place of *quien* or *quienes* in this sense, you can also use *el que, la que, los que, las que.*

Quien escucha oye. / Who listens hears. He who listens hears. She who listens hears.

OR:

El que escucha oye. / He who listens hears.
La que escucha oye. / She who listens hears.
Quienes escuchan oyen. / Who listen hear. Those who listen hear. The ones who listen hear.

OR:

Los que escuchan oyen. Las que escuchan oyen. / Those who listen hear.

• As subject of a verb, the relative pronoun *quien* may be used instead of *que* referring only to persons when it is subject of a nonrestrictive dependent clause set off by commas:

La señora Gómez, quien (or que) es profesora, conoce a mi madre / Mrs. Gómez, who is a teacher, knows my mother.

• As direct object of a verb referring only to persons, the relative pronoun *quien* or *quienes* may be used with the personal *a (a quien, a quienes)* instead of *que:*

La muchacha que (or a quien) Ud. vio al baile es mi hermana / The girl whom you saw at the dance is my sister.

- As object of a preposition referring only to persons:

  ¿Conoces a la chica con quien tomé el almuerzo? / Do you
  know the girl with whom I had lunch?
  ¿Conoces a los chicos con quienes María tomó el almuerzo? /
  Do you know the boys with whom Mary had lunch?
  ¿Conoce Ud. a los hombres de quienes hablo? / Do you know
  the men of whom (about whom) I am talking?

§6.5–3 *el cual, la cual, los cuales, las cuales* / who, that, whom, which, the one which, the ones which, the one who, the ones who

These relative pronouns may be used in place of *que* to clarify the gender and number of *que:*

  La madre de José, la cual es muy inteligente, es dentista /
  Joseph's mother, who is very intelligent, is a dentist.

These substitute relative pronouns may also refer to things:

  El libro, el cual está sobre la mesa, es mío / The book, which is
  on the table, is mine.

These relative pronouns are also used as substitutes for *el que, la que, los que, las que* when used as the subject of a nonrestrictive dependent clause set off by commas:

  La señora Gómez, la cual (or *la que,* or *quien,* or *que*) *es
  profesora, conoce a mi madre* / Mrs. Gómez, who is a teacher,
  knows my mother.

These relative pronouns, as well as *el que, la que, los que, las que,* are used as objects of prepositions except with *a, con, de, en* — in which case the relative pronoun *que* is preferred with things. These relative pronouns *(el cual, la cual, los cuales, las cuales* and *el que, la que, los que, las que)* are commonly used with the following prepositions: *para, por, sin, delante de, cerca de,* and *sobre:*

  *En este cuarto, hay una gran ventana por la cual se ve el sol
  por la mañana* / In this room, there is a large window through
  which you (one, anyone) can see the sun in the morning.

These compound relative pronouns refer to persons as well as things and can be used as subject of a verb or direct object of a verb when used in a nonrestrictive dependent clause separated from its antecedent and set off with commas.

§6.5 – 4 *lo cual* / which; *lo que* / what, that which

These are neuter compound relative pronouns. They do not refer to an antecedent of any gender or number.

Lo cual and *lo que* refer to a statement, a clause, an idea:

Mi hijo Juan estudia sus lecciones todos los días, lo cual es bueno / My son John studies his lessons every day, which is good.

Mi hija recibió buenas notas, lo que me gustó / My daughter received good marks, which pleased me.

Lo que is also used to express "what" in the sense of "that which:"

Comprendo lo que Ud. dice / I understand what (that which) you say.

Lo que Ud. dice es verdad / What (That which) you say is true.

§6.5 – 5 *cuanto* = *todo lo que* / all that

As a relative pronoun, *cuanto* may be used in place of *todo lo que:*

Todo lo que Ud. dice es verdad;

OR

Cuanto Ud. dice es verdad / All that (All that which) you say is true.

§6.5 – 6 *cuyo, cuya, cuyos, cuyas* / whose

This word (and its forms as given) refers to persons and things. Strictly speaking, *cuyo,* etc. is not regarded as a relative pronoun but rather as a relative possessive adjective. It agrees in gender and number with what is possessed (whose . . .), not with the possessor. Its position is directly in front of the noun it modifies.

El señor García, cuyos hijos son inteligentes, es profesor / Mr. García, whose children are intelligent, is a professor.

El muchacho, cuya madre es profesora, es inteligente / The boy, whose mother is a professor, is intelligent.

> The forms of *cuyo* cannot be used as an interrogative when you ask "Whose is . . . ?" You must use *de quién: ¿De quién es este libro?*

When referring to parts of the body, use *a quien* instead of *cuyo:*

> *La niña, a quien la madre lavó las manos, es bonita* / The child, whose hands the mother washed, is pretty.

§6.6 Interrogative Pronouns

See also specific interrogatives (*qué, cuál,* etc.) in the index.

Here are a few common interrogatives that you should be aware of. Note the required accent mark on these words when used in a question.

¿qué . . . ? / what . . . ?
¿cuál . . . ? / which, which one . . . ?
¿cuáles . . . ? / which, which ones . . . ?
¿quién . . . ? ¿quiénes . . . ? / who . . . ?
¿a quién . . . ? ¿a quiénes . . . ? / whom . . . ? to
                                        whom . . . ?
¿de quién . . . ? / of whom, from whom, by whom,
                             whose . . . ?
¿De quién es este lápiz? / Whose is this pencil?

---

§6.7 Indefinite Pronouns

algo / something, anything
(with *sin*, use *nada: sin nada* / without anything)
alguien / anybody, anyone, someone, somebody
(with *sin*, use *nadie: sin nadie* / without anyone)
alguno, alguna, algunos, algunas / some, any

§6.8 Negative Pronouns

nada / nothing: *sin nada* / without anything
(after *sin, nada* is used instead of *algo: Ella no quiere nada* /
    She does not want anything.)
nadie / nobody, no one, not anyone, not anybody: *sin nadie* /
    without anybody
(after *sin, nadie* is used instead of *alguien*)
ninguno, ninguna / no one, none, not any, not anybody

§7.
Verbs

§7.1
AGREEMENT

§7.1–1
Subject and Verb

A subject and verb form must agree in person and number. By person is meant 1st, 2nd, or 3rd; by number is meant singular or plural. To get a picture of the three persons in the singular and in the plural, see subject pronouns in §6.

§7.1–2
Subject and Reflexive Pronoun of a Reflexive Verb

A subject and reflexive pronoun must agree in person and number. To get a picture of the correct reflexive pronoun that goes with the subject, according to the person you need (1st, 2nd or 3rd, singular or plural), see reflexive pronouns in §6.

§7.2
TYPES

§7.2–1
Auxiliary (or helping) Verb *haber* (to have)

The auxiliary (helping) verb *haber* is used in any of the seven simple tenses + the past participle of the main verb to form the seven compound tenses.

§7.2–2
Transitive Verbs

A transitive verb is a verb that takes a direct object. It is transitive because the action passes over from the subject and directly affects someone or something in some way.

> *Veo a mi amigo.* / I see my friend.
> *Abro la ventana.* / I open the window.

When the direct object of the verb is a pronoun, it is placed in front of the verb most of the time; at other times it is attached to an infinitive; if the main verb is *poder, querer, saber, ir a* + infinitive, the direct object pronoun may be placed in front of the main verb instead of attaching it to the infinitive; at other times, the direct object pronoun is attached to a present participle. For an in-depth analysis of the word order of elements in Spanish sentences, particularly pronouns, review §6.

Here are the same sentences as above, but with direct object pronouns instead of direct object nouns:

> *(Yo) le veo.* / I see him.
> *(Yo) la abro.* / I open it.

For the position of pronouns in other types of sentences in Spanish, review position of object pronouns in §6.

§7.2–3 Intransitive Verbs

An intransitive verb is a verb that does not take a direct object. It is called intransitive because the action does not pass over from the subject and directly affect anyone or anything.

> *La profesora está hablando.* / The teacher is talking.
> *La señora Gómez salió temprano.* / Mrs. Gómez left early.

An intransitive verb takes an indirect object.

> *La profesora está hablando a los alumnos* / The teacher is talking to the students.

The indirect object noun is *alumnos* because it is preceded by *a los* (to the).

> *La profesora les está hablando.* / The teacher is talking to them.

The indirect object is the pronoun *les,* to them.

For a review of direct object pronouns and indirect object pronouns, see §6.

A transitive verb can take an indirect object.

> *La profesora da los libros a los alumnos.* / The teacher is giving the books to the pupils.

The direct object is *los libros;* the indirect object is *a los alumnos.*

> *La profesora los da a los alumnos.* / The teacher is giving them to the pupils.

The direct object pronoun is *los* (meaning *los libros*) and the indirect object noun is still *a los alumnos.*

> *La profesora les da los libros.* / The teacher is giving the books to them.

The indirect object pronoun is *les* (meaning "to them," i.e., *a los alumnos*).

> *La profesora se los da.* / The teacher is giving them to them.

The indirect object pronoun *les* changes to *se* because *les* is 3rd person and it is followed by *los,* a direct object pronoun, which is also 3rd person. For a review of this point in Spanish grammar, see position of double object pronouns in §6.

You may clarify the indirect object pronoun *se* in this sentence by adding *a ellos* or *a los alumnos.*

§7.3
PARTICIPLES

§7.3–1
Past Participle

A past participle is regularly formed as follows:

Infinitive	Drop	Add	To the Stem	You Get
trabajar	-ar	ado	*trabaj*	*trabajado*
comer	-er	ido	*com*	*comido*
recibir	-ir	ido	*recib*	*recibido*

COMMON IRREGULAR PAST PARTICIPLES

Infinitive	Past Participle
abrir / to open	*abierto* / opened
caer / to fall	*caído* / fallen
creer / to believe	*creído* / believed
cubrir / to cover	*cubierto* / covered
decir / to say, to tell	*dicho* / said, told
devolver / to return (something)	*devuelto* / returned (something)
escribir / to write	*escrito* / written
hacer / to do, to make	*hecho* / done, made
ir / to go	*ido* / gone
leer / to read	*leído* / read
morir / to die	*muerto* / died
oír / to hear	*oído* / heard
poner / to put	*puesto* / put
reír / to laugh	*reído* / laughed
resolver / to resolve, to solve	*resuelto* / resolved, solved
romper / to break	*roto* / broken
traer / to bring	*traído* / brought
ver / to see	*visto* / seen
volver / to return	*vuelto* / returned

Uses of the Past Participle

To form the compound tenses:

As in English, the past participle is needed to form the compound tenses in Spanish, of which there are seven. For the complete conjugation showing the forms of the six persons in each of the following compound tenses and for an explanation of how they are formed, see the specific name of each tense in the index.

THE COMPOUND TENSES	
Name of tense	**Example (1st person, singular)**
Present Perfect Indicative	*he hablado*
Pluperfect Indicative	*había hablado*
Preterit Perfect	*hube hablado*
Future Perfect	*habré hablado*
Conditional Perfect	*habría hablado*
Present Perfect Subjunctive	*haya hablado*
Pluperfect Subjunctive	*hubiera hablado* or *hubiese hablado*

To form the Perfect Infinitive:

haber hablado / to have spoken

To form the Perfect Participle:

habiendo hablado / having spoken

To serve as an adjective, which must agree in gender and number with the noun it modifies:

El señor Molina es muy respetado de todos los alumnos. / Mr. Molina is very respected by all the students.
La señora González es muy conocida. / Mrs. González is very well known.

To express the result of an action with *estar:*

La puerta está abierta. / The door is open.
Las cartas están escritas. / The letters are written.

To express the passive voice with *ser:*

La ventana fue abierta por el ladrón. / The window was opened by the robber.

§7.3 – 2 Present Participle

A present participle is a verb form which, in English, ends in -ing: singing, eating, receiving. In Spanish, a present participle is regularly formed as follows:

drop the *ar* of an *-ar* ending verb, like *cantar,* and add *-ando:*
cantando / singing
drop the *er* of an *-er* ending verb, like *comer,* and add *-iendo:*
comiendo / eating
drop the *ir* of an *-ir* ending verb, like *recibir,* and add *-iendo:*
recibiendo / receiving

Gerunds and Present Participles

In English, a gerund also ends in -ing but there is a distinct difference in use between a gerund and a present participle. When a present participle is used as a noun it is called a gerund; for example: Reading is good. As a present participle: The boy fell asleep while reading.

In the first example (Reading is good), reading is a gerund because it is the subject of the verb "is." In Spanish, however, we must not use the present participle form as a noun to serve as a subject; we must use the infinitive form of the verb: *Leer es bueno.*

COMMON IRREGULAR PRESENT PARTICIPLES

Infinitive	**Present Participle**
caer / to fall	*cayendo* / falling
construir / to construct	*construyendo* / constructing
corregir / to correct	*corrigiendo* / correcting
creer / to believe	*creyendo* / believing
decir / to say, to tell	*diciendo* / saying, telling
despedirse / to say good-bye	*despidiéndose* / saying good-bye
divertirse / to enjoy oneself	*divirtiéndose* / enjoying oneself
dormir / to sleep	*durmiendo* / sleeping
ir / to go	*yendo* / going
leer / to read	*leyendo* / reading
mentir / to lie (tell a falsehood)	*mintiendo* / lying
morir / to die	*muriendo* / dying
oír / to hear	*oyendo* / hearing
pedir / to ask (for), to request	*pidiendo* / asking (for), requesting
poder / to be able	*pudiendo* / being able
reír / to laugh	*riendo* / laughing
repetir / to repeat	*repitiendo* / repeating
seguir / to follow	*siguiendo* / following
sentir / to feel	*sintiendo* / feeling
servir / to serve	*sirviendo* / serving
traer / to bring	*trayendo* / bringing
venir / to come	*viniendo* / coming
vestir / to dress	*vistiendo* / dressing

Uses of the Present Participle

To form the progressive tenses:

The progressive present is formed by using *estar* in the present tense plus the present participle of the main verb you are using.

Estoy hablando. / I am talking.

The progressive past is formed by using *estar* in the imperfect indicative plus the present participle of the main verb you are using.

Estaba hablando. / I was talking.

Instead of using *estar,* as noted above, to form these two progressive tenses, sometimes *ir* is used:

Va hablando. / He (she) keeps right on talking.
Iba hablando. / He (she) kept right on talking.

To express vividly an action that occurred (preterit + present participle):

El niño entró llorando en la casa. / The little boy came crying into the house.

To express the English use of "by" + present participle in Spanish, we use the gerund form, which has the same ending as a present participle.

Trabajando se gana dinero. / By working, one earns (a person earns) money.
Estudiando mucho, Pepe recibió buenas notas. / By studying hard, Joe received good grades.

No preposition is used in front of the present participle (the Spanish gerund) even though it is expressed in English as "by" + present participle.

In Spanish we use *al* + infinitive (not + present participle) to express "on" or "upon" + present participle:

Al entrar en la casa, el niño comenzó a llorar. / Upon entering the house, the little boy began to cry.

To form the perfect participle:

habiendo hablado / having talked

V

§7.4
VERBS AND PREPOSITIONS

A verb right after a preposition is in the infinitive form:

Pablo salió sin hablar. / Paul went out without talking.

§7.4–1
Verbs of Motion Take the Preposition *a* + Infinitive

ir a / to go to
regresar a / to return to
salir a / to go out to
venir a / to come to
volver a / to return to

EXAMPLE:

> *María fue a comer.* / Mary went to eat.

§7.4–2
Verbs That Take the Preposition *a* + Infinitive

aprender a / to learn to, to learn how to
aspirar a / to aspire to
ayudar a (hacer algo) / to help to
comenzar a / to begin to
decidirse a / to decide to
dedicarse a / to devote oneself to
detenerse a / to pause to, to stop to
empezar a / to begin to, to start to
enseñar a / to teach to
invitar a / to invite to
negarse a / to refuse to
ponerse a / to begin to, to start to
prepararse a / to prepare (oneself) to
principiar a / to begin to, to start to
venir a / to end up by
volver a / to do something again

EXAMPLES:

> *El señor Gómez se negó a ir.* / Mr. Gómez refused to go.
> *Juana se puso a correr.* / Jane began to run.
> *El muchacho volvió a jugar.* / The boy played again.

§7.4–3
Verbs That Take the Preposition *a* + Noun (or Pronoun)

acercarse a / to approach
asistir a / to attend, to be present at
asomarse a / to appear at
dar a / to face, to overlook, to look out upon, to look out over
dedicarse a / to devote oneself to
echar una carta al correo / to mail, to post a letter
jugar a / to play (a game, sport, cards)

llegar a ser / to become
querer a / to love
ser aficionado a / to be fond of, to be a fan of
subir a / to get on, to get into (a bus, a train, a vehicle)

EXAMPLES:

Nos acercamos a la ciudad. / We are approaching the city.
Una muchacha bonita se asomó a la puerta. / A pretty girl
    appeared at the door.
Mi cuarto da al jardín. / My room faces the garden.
Me dedico a mis estudios. / I devote myself to my studies.

§7.4–4 Verbs That Take the Preposition *con* + Infinitive

contar con / to count on, to rely on
soñar con / to dream of, to dream about

EXAMPLES:

Cuento con tener éxito. / I am counting on being successful.
Sueño con ir a Chile. / I dream of going to Chile.

§7.4–5 Verbs That Take the Preposition *con* + Noun (or Pronoun)

casarse con / to marry, to get married to
cumplir con / to fulfill
dar con / to meet, to find, to come upon
encontrarse con / to run into, to meet by chance

EXAMPLE:

José se casó con Ana. / Joseph married Anna.

§7.4–6 Verbs That Take the Preposition *de* + Infinitive

acabar de / to have just
acordarse de / to remember to
alegrarse de / to be glad to
cansarse de / to become tired of
dejar de / to stop, to fail to
ocuparse de / to be busy with, to attend to
olvidarse de / to forget to
tratar de / to try to

EXAMPLES:

Guillermo acaba de llegar. / William has just arrived.
Me alegro de hablarle. / I am glad to talk to you.
Me canso de esperar el autobús. / I'm getting tired of
                           waiting for the bus.

§7.4−7
Verbs That Take the Preposition *de* + Noun (or Pronoun)

acordarse de / to remember
aprovecharse de / to take advantage of
bajar de / to get out of, to descend from, to get off
burlarse de / to make fun of
cambiar de / to change (trains, buses, clothes, etc.)
cansarse de / to become tired of

EXAMPLES:

Me acuerdo de aquel hombre. / I remember that man.
Vamos a aprovecharnos de esta oportunidad. / Let's take advantage of this opportunity.
Después de bajar del tren, fui a comer. / After getting off the train, I went to eat.
Todos los días cambio de ropa. / Every day I change my clothes.
Me canso de este trabajo. / I am getting tired of this work.

§7.4−8
Verbs That Generally Take the Preposition *en* + Infinitive

consentir en / to consent to
convenir en / to agree to, to agree on
empeñarse en / to persist in, to insist on
insistir en / to insist on
quedar en / to agree to, to agree on
tardar en / to be late (to delay) in

EXAMPLES:

El muchacho se empeñó en salir. / The boy insisted on going out.
El avión tardó en llegar. / The plane was late in arriving.

§7.4−9
Verbs That Generally Take the Preposition *en* + Noun (or Pronoun)

apoyarse en / to lean against, to lean on
confiar en / to rely on, to trust in
consistir en / to consist of
entrar en / to enter (into), to go into
fijarse en / to stare at, to notice, to take notice, to observe
pensar en / to think of, to think about (*pensar en* is used when asking or when stating what or whom a person is thinking of)
ponerse en camino / to set out, to start out

EXAMPLES:

Me apoyé en la puerta. / I leaned against the door.
Entré en el restaurante. / I entered (I went in) the restaurant.
¿En qué piensa Ud.? / What are you thinking of?
Pienso en mi trabajo. / I am thinking of my work.

§7.4–10
Verbs That Generally Take the Preposition *por* + Infinitive, Noun, Pronoun, Adjective

acabar por / to end up by
dar por / to consider, to regard as
darse por / to pretend (to be something), to think oneself (to be something)
estar por / to be in favor of
interesarse por / to take an interest in
preguntar por / to ask for, to inquire about

EXAMPLES:

Domingo acabó por casarse con Elena. / Dominic finally ended up by marrying Helen.
¿Mi libro de español? Lo doy por perdido. / My Spanish book? I consider it lost.
La señorita López se da por actriz. / Miss López pretends to be an actress.

§7.4–11
Verb + no Preposition + Infinitive.

deber + infinitive / must, ought to

Debo hacer mis lecciones. / I must (ought to) do my lessons.

Verbs That Do Not Ordinarily Take a Preposition When Followed by an Infinitive

decidir + infinitive / to decide
dejar + infinitive / to allow to, to let

Mi madre me dejó salir. / My mother allowed me to go out.
Dejé caer mi libro. / I dropped my book (I let my book fall).

desear + infinitive / to desire to, to wish to

Deseo tomar un café. / I wish to have a cup of coffee.

esperar + infinitive / to expect to, to hope to

Espero ir a la América del Sur este invierno. / I expect to go to South America this winter.

hacer + infinitive / to do, to make, to have something made or done

Tú me haces reír. / You make me laugh.

necesitar + infinitive / to need

> *Necesito pasar una hora en la biblioteca.* / I need to spend an hour in the library.

oír + infinitive / to hear

> *Le oí entrar por la ventana.* / I heard him enter through the window.

pensar + infinitive / to intend to, to plan to

> *Pienso hacer un viaje a México.* / I plan to take a trip to Mexico.

poder + infinitive / to be able to, can

> *Puedo venir a verle a la una.* / I can come to see you at one o'clock.

preferir + infinitive / to prefer

> *Prefiero quedarme en casa esta noche.* / I prefer to stay at home this evening.

prometer + infinitive / to promise

> *Prometo venir a verle a las ocho.* / I promise to come to see you at eight o'clock.

querer + infinitive / to want to, to wish to

> *Quiero comer ahora.* / I want to eat now.

saber + infinitive / to know how to

> *¿Sabe Ud. nadar?* / Do you know how to swim?
> *Sí, yo sé nadar.* / Yes, I know how to swim.

ver + infinitive / to see

> *Veo venir el tren.* / I see the train coming.

§7.4–12
Verbs That Do Not Ordinarily Require a Preposition, Whereas in English a Preposition is Used

buscar / to look for, to search for

> *Busco mi libro.* / I am looking for my book.

escuchar / to listen to

> *Escucho la música.* / I am listening to the music.

esperar / to wait for

> *Espero el autobús.* / I am waiting for the bus.

guardar cama / to stay in bed

> *La semana pasada guardé cama.* / Last week I stayed in bed.

mirar / to look at

> *Miro el cielo.* / I am looking at the sky.

pagar / to pay for

> *Pagué los billetes.* / I paid for the tickets.

pedir / to ask for

> *Pido un libro.* / I am asking for a book.

§7.5
TENSES AND MOODS

§7.5–1
Present Indicative

This tense is used most of the time in Spanish and English. It indicates:

● An action or a state of being at the present time.

EXAMPLES:

> *Hablo español.* / I speak Spanish.
> *Creo en Dios.* / I believe in God.

- Habitual action.

  EXAMPLE:

  > *Voy a la biblioteca todos los días.* / I go to the library every day.

- A general truth, something which is permanently true.

  EXAMPLE:

  > *Seis menos dos son cuatro.* / Six minus two are four.

- Vividness when talking or writing about past events.

  EXAMPLE:

  > *El asesino se pone pálido. Tiene miedo. Sale de la casa y corre a lo largo del río.* / The murderer turns pale. He is afraid. He goes out of the house and runs along the river.

- A near future.

  EXAMPLE:

  > *Mi hermano llega mañana.* / My brother arrives tomorrow.

- An action or state of being that occurred in the past and continues up to the present. In Spanish this is an idiomatic use of the present tense of a verb with *hace,* which is also in the present.

  EXAMPLE:

  > *Hace tres horas que miro la televisión.* / I have been watching television for three hours.

- The meaning of "almost" or "nearly" when used with *por poco.*

  EXAMPLE:

  > *Por poco me matan.* / They almost killed me.

This tense is regularly formed as follows:

Drop the *ar* ending of an infinitive, like *hablar,* and add: *o, as, a; amos, áis, an.*

You then get: *hablo, hablas, habla;*
hablamos, habláis, hablan.

Drop the *er* ending of an infinitive, like *beber,* and add:
o, es, e; emos, éis, en.

You then get: *bebo, bebes, bebe;*
bebemos, bebéis, beben.

Drop the *ir* ending of an infinitive, like *recibir,* and add:
o, es, e; imos, ís, en.

You then get: *recibo, recibes, recibe;*
recibimos, recibís, reciben.

§7.5–2 Imperfect Indicative

This is a past tense. Imperfect suggests incomplete. The Imperfect tense expresses an action or a state of being that was continuous in the past and its completion is not indicated. It expresses:

- An action that was going on in the past at the same time as another action.

  EXAMPLE:

  > *Mi hermano leía y mi padre hablaba.* / My brother was reading and my father was talking.

- An action that was going on in the past when another action occurred.

  EXAMPLE:

  > *Mi hermana cantaba cuando yo entré.* / My sister was singing when I came in.

- An action that a person did habitually in the past.

  EXAMPLE:

  > *Cuando estábamos en Nueva York, íbamos al cine todos los sábados.* / When we were in New York, we went to the movies every Saturday; When we were in New York, we used to go to the movies every Saturday.

- A description of a mental, emotional, or physical condition in the past.

EXAMPLES:

> (mental condition)   *Quería ir al cine.* / I wanted to go to the movies.
>
> (emotional condition)   *Estaba contento de verlo.* / I was happy to see him.
>
> (physical condition)   *Mi madre era hermosa cuando era pequeña.* / My mother was beautiful when she was young.

- The time of day in the past.

  EXAMPLES:

  > *¿Qué hora era?* / What time was it?
  > *Eran las tres.* / It was three o'clock.

- An action or state of being that occurred in the past and lasted for a certain length of time prior to another past action.

  EXAMPLE:

  > *Hacía tres horas que miraba la televisión cuando mi hermano entró.* / I had been watching television for three hours when my brother came in.

- An indirect quotation in the past.

  EXAMPLE:

  > Present: *Dice que quiere venir a mi casa.* / He says he wants to come to my house.
  > Past: *Dijo que quería venir a mi casa.* / He said he wanted to come to my house.

This tense is regularly formed as follows:

Drop the -*ar* ending of an infinitive, like *hablar,* and add: *aba, abas, aba; ábamos, abais, aban*

You then get: *hablaba, hablabas, hablaba; hablábamos, hablabais, hablaban.*

The usual equivalent in English is: I was talking, I used to talk, I talked.

Drop the -*er* ending of an infinitive, like *beber,* or the -*ir* ending of an infinitive, like *recibir,* and add: *ía, ías, ía; íamos, íais, ían*

You then get: *bebía, bebías, bebía; bebíamos, bebíais, bebían.*

The usual equivalent in English is: I was drinking, I used to drink, I drank.

§7.5 – 3
Preterit

This tense expresses an action that was completed at some time in the past.

EXAMPLES:

Mi padre llegó ayer. / My father arrived yesterday.
María fue a la iglesia esta mañana. / Mary went to church
  this morning.
¿Qué pasó? / What happened?
Tomé el desayuno a las siete. / I had breakfast at seven
  o'clock.
*Salí de casa, tomé el autobús y llegué a la escuela a las
ocho.* / I left the house, I took the bus and I arrived at school
  at eight o'clock.

In Spanish, some verbs have a different meaning when used in the preterit.

EXAMPLES:

La conocí la semana pasada en el baile. / I met her last
  week at the dance.
Pude hacerlo. / I succeeded in doing it.
No pude hacerlo. / I failed to do it.
Quise llamarlo. / I tried to call you.
No quise hacerlo. / I refused to do it.
Supe la verdad. / I found out the truth.
Tuve una carta de mi amigo Roberto. / I received a letter
  from my friend Robert.

This tense is regularly formed as follows:

- Drop the *-ar* ending of an infinitive, like *hablar,* and add:
  é, aste, ó; amos, asteis, aron.
      You then get: *hablé, hablaste, habló,*
                    hablamos, hablasteis, hablaron.

    The usual equivalent in English is: I talked, I did talk; you talked, you did talk, etc. I spoke, I did speak; you spoke, you did speak, etc.

- Drop the *-er* ending of an infinitive, like *beber,* or the *-ir* ending of an infinitive, like *recibir,* and add:
  í, iste, ió; imos, isteis, ieron.
      You then get: *bebí, bebiste, bebió,*
                    bebimos, bebisteis, bebieron.

§7.5 – 4
Future

In Spanish and English, the future tense is used to express an action or a state of being that will take place at some time in the future.

Lo haré. / I shall do it; I will do it.

Also, in Spanish the future tense is used to indicate:

- Conjecture regarding the present.

  ¿Qué hora será? / I wonder what time it is.
  ¿Quién será? / Who can that be? I wonder who that is.

- Probability regarding the present.

  Serán las cinco. / It is probably five o'clock; It must be five o'clock.
  Tendrá muchos amigos. / He probably has many friends; He must have many friends.

- An indirect quotation.

  María dice que vendrá mañana. / Mary says that she will come tomorrow.

Remember that the future is never used in Spanish after *si* when *si* means "if."
This tense is regularly formed as follows:
Add the following endings to the whole infinitive:
é, ás, á; emos, éis, án.
You then get: *hablaré, hablarás, hablará, hablaremos, hablaréis, hablarán.*

§7.5 – 5
Conditional

The conditional is used in Spanish and in English to express:

- An action that you would do if something else were possible.

  Iría a España si tuviera dinero. / I would go to Spain if I had money.

- A conditional desire. This is a conditional of courtesy.

  Me gustaría tomar una limonada. / I would like to have a lemonade.

- An indirect quotation.

  María dijo que vendría mañana. / Mary said that she would come tomorrow.
  María decía que vendría mañana. / Mary was saying that she would come tomorrow.

- Conjecture regarding the past.

  ¿Quién sería? / I wonder who that was.

- Probability regarding the past.

  Serían las cinco cuando salieron. / It was probably five o'clock
  when they went out.

This tense is regularly formed as follows:

Add the following endings to the whole infinitive:
ía, ías, ía; íamos, íais, ían.

You then get: *hablaría, hablarías, hablaría,
hablaríamos, hablaríais, hablarían.*

**§7.5 – 6
Present
Subjunctive**

The subjunctive mood is used in Spanish much more than
in English. In Spanish the present subjunctive is used:

- To express a command in the *usted* or *ustedes* form, either
  in the affirmative or negative.

  Siéntese Ud. / Sit down.
  No se siente Ud. / Don't sit down.

- To express a negative command in the familiar form *(tú).*

  No te sientes. / Don't sit down.
  No duermas. / Don't sleep.

- To express a command in the first person plural, either in
  the affirmative or negative *(nosotros).*

  Sentémonos. / Let's sit down.
  No entremos. / Let's not go in.

- After a verb that expresses some kind of wish, insistence,
  preference, suggestion, or request.

  Quiero que María lo haga. / I want Mary to do it.
  Insisto en que María lo haga. / I insist that Mary do it.

- After a verb that expresses doubt, fear, joy, hope, sorrow,
  or some other emotion.

  Dudo que María lo haga. / I doubt that Mary is doing it; I doubt
  that Mary will do it.
  No creo que María venga. / I don't believe (I doubt) that Mary is
  coming; I don't believe (I doubt)
  that Mary will come.

- After certain impersonal expressions that show necessity,
  doubt, regret, importance, urgency, or possibility.

  Es necesario que María lo haga. / It is necessary for Mary to do
  it; It is necessary that Mary
  do it.

No es cierto que María venga. / It is doubtful (not certain) that Mary is coming; It is doubtful (not certain) that Mary will come.

- After certain conjunctions of time, such as *antes (de) que, cuando, en cuanto, después (de) que, hasta que, mientras,* and the like.

    Le hablaré a María cuando venga. / I shall talk to Mary when she comes.

    Vámonos antes (de) que llueva. / Let's go before it rains.

- After certain conjunctions that express a condition, negation, purpose, such as *a menos que, con tal que, para que, a fin de que, sin que, en caso (de) que,* and the like.

    Démelo con tal que sea bueno. / Give it to me provided that it is good.

    Me voy a menos que venga. / I'm leaving unless he comes.

- After certain adverbs, such as *acaso, quizá,* and *tal vez.*

    Acaso venga mañana. / Perhaps he will come tomorrow. Perhaps he is coming tomorrow.

- After *aunque* if the action has not yet occurred.

    Aunque María venga esta noche, no me quedo. / Although Mary may come tonight, I'm not staying; Although Mary is coming tonight, I'm not staying.

- In an adjectival clause if the antecedent is something or someone that is indefinite, negative, vague, or nonexistent.

    Busco un libro que sea interesante. / I'm looking for a book that is interesting.
    ¿Hay alguien aquí que hable francés? / Is there anyone here who speaks French?
    No hay nadie que pueda hacerlo. / There is no one who can do it.

- After *por más que* or *por mucho que.*

    Por más que hable usted, no quiero escuchar. / No matter how much you talk, I don't want to listen.

- After the expression *ojalá (que),* which expresses a great desire. This interjection means "would to God!" or "may God grant!" It is derived from the Arabic.

    ¡Ojalá que vengan mañana! / Would to God that they come tomorrow!

Finally, remember that the present subjunctive is never used in Spanish after *si* when *si* means "if."

The present subjunctive of regular verbs and many irregular verbs is normally formed as follows:

Go to the present indicative, 1st person singular of the verb you have in mind, drop the ending *o*, and

- for an *-ar* ending type, add: *e, es, e; emos, éis, en*
- for an *-er* or *-ir* ending type, add: *a, as, a; amos, áis, an*

You then get, for example: *hable, hables, hable; hablemos, habléis, hablen*

beba, bebas, beba; bebamos, bebáis, beban

reciba, recibas, reciba; recibamos, recibáis, reciban

§7.5–7 Imperfect Subjunctive

This past tense is used for the same reasons as the *presente de subjuntivo* — that is, after certain verbs, conjunctions, impersonal expressions, etc., which were explained and illustrated above. The main difference between these two tenses is the time of the action.

If the verb in the main clause is in the present indicative or future or present perfect indicative or imperative, the present subjunctive or the present perfect subjunctive is used in the dependent clause — provided, of course, that there is some element which requires the use of the subjunctive.

However, if the verb in the main clause is in the imperfect indicative, preterit, conditional, or pluperfect indicative, the imperfect subjunctive (this tense) or pluperfect subjunctive is ordinarily used in the dependent clause — provided, of course, that there is some element which requires the use of the subjunctive.

EXAMPLES:
Insistí en que María lo hiciera. / I insisted that Mary do it.
Se lo explicaba a María para que lo comprendiera. / I was explaining it to Mary so that she might understand it.

Note that the imperfect subjunctive is used after *como si* to express a condition contrary to fact.

EXAMPLE:
Me habla como si fuera un niño. / He speaks to me as if I were a child.

Finally, note that *quisiera* (the imperfect subjunctive of *querer*) can be used to express in a very polite way, I would like:

Quisiera hablar ahora. / I would like to speak now.

The imperfect subjunctive is regularly formed as follows:
For all verbs, drop the *-ron* ending of the 3rd person plural of the preterit and add the following endings:

ra, ras, ra; *ramos, rais, ran*	OR	*se, ses, se;* *semos, seis, sen*

EXAMPLES:

Preterit, 3rd Person Plural	Imperfect Subjunctive
bebieron (beber)	*bebiera, bebieras, bebiera;* *bebiéramos, bebierais, bebieran* OR *bebiese, bebieses, bebiese;* *bebiésemos, bebieseis, bebiesen*
dijeron (decir)	*dijera, dijeras, dijera;* *dijéramos, dijerais, dijeran* OR *dijese, dijeses, dijese;* *dijésemos, dijeseis, dijesen*
fueron (ir)	*fuera, fueras, fuera;* *fuéramos, fuerais, fueran* OR *fuese, fueses, fuese;* *fuésemos, fueseis, fuesen*

§7.5–8 Present Perfect Indicative

This tense expresses an action that took place at no definite time in the past. It is a compound tense because it is formed with the present indicative of *haber* (the auxiliary or helping verb) plus the past participle of the verb you have in mind.

(Yo) he hablado. / I have spoken.
(Tú) no has venido a verme. / You have not come to see me.
Elena ha ganado el premio. / Helen has won the prize.

§7.5–9 Pluperfect OR Past Perfect Indicative

In Spanish and English, this past tense is used to express an action which happened in the past before another past action. Since it is used in relation to another past action, the other past action is ordinarily expressed in the preterit.

In Spanish, this tense is formed with the imperfect indicative of *haber* plus the past participle of the verb you have in mind.

Cuando llegué a casa, mi hermano había salido. / **When I arrived home, my brother had gone out.**
Juan lo había perdido en la calle. / **John had lost it in the street.**

§7.5–10
Past Anterior
OR Preterit
Perfect

This past tense is compound because it is formed with the preterit of *haber* plus the past participle of the verb you are using. It is translated into English like the pluperfect indicative explained above.

This tense is ordinarily used in formal writing, such as history and literature. It is normally used after certain conjunctions of time, e.g., *después que, cuando, apenas, luego que, en cuanto.*

EXAMPLE:
Después que hubo hablado, salió. / **After he had spoken, he left.**

§7.5–11
Future Perfect
OR Future
Anterior

This compound tense is formed with the future of *haber* plus the past participle of the verb you have in mind. In Spanish and in English, this tense is used to express an action that will happen in the future before another future action. In English, this tense is formed by using "shall have" or "will have" plus the past participle of the verb you have in mind.

EXAMPLE:
María llegará mañana y habré terminado mi trabajo. / **Mary will arrive tomorrow and I will have finished my work.**

Also, in Spanish the future perfect is used to indicate conjecture or probability regarding recent past time.

EXAMPLES:
María se habrá acostado. / **Mary has probably gone to bed; Mary must have gone to bed.**
José habrá llegado. / **Joseph has probably arrived; Joseph must have arrived.**

§7.5–12
Conditional
Perfect

This is formed with the conditional of *haber* plus the past participle of the verb you have in mind. It is used in Spanish and English to express an action that you would have done if something else had been possible; that is, you would have done something on condition that something else had been possible.

In English it is formed by using would have plus the past participle of the verb you have in mind.

EXAMPLE:

Habría ido a España si hubiera tenido dinero. / I would have gone to Spain if I had had money.

Also, in Spanish the conditional perfect is used to indicate probability or conjecture in the past.

EXAMPLES:

Habrían sido las cinco cuando salieron. / It must have been five o'clock when they went out.

¿Quién habría sido? / Who could that have been? (or I wonder who that could have been).

§7.5–13 Present Perfect OR Past Subjunctive

This is formed by using the present subjunctive of *haber* as the helping verb plus the past participle of the verb you have in mind.

María duda que yo le haya hablado al profesor. / Mary doubts that I have spoken to the professor.

Siento que tú no hayas venido a verme. / I am sorry that you have not come to see me.

§7.5–14 Pluperfect OR Past Perfect Subjunctive

This is formed by using the imperfect subjunctive of *haber* as the helping verb plus the past participle of the verb you have in mind.

EXAMPLES:

Sentí mucho que no hubiera venido María. / I was very sorry that Mary had not come.

Me alegraba de que hubiera venido María. / I was glad that Mary had come.

§7.5–15 Progressive Forms of Tenses

• In Spanish, there are also progressive forms of tenses. They are the progressive present and the progressive past.
• The progressive present is formed by using *estar* in the present tense plus the present participle of your main verb: *Estoy hablando* (I am talking).
• The progressive past is formed by using *estar* in the imperfect indicative plus the present participle of your main verb: *Estaba hablando* (I was talking).
• The progressive forms are used when you want to emphasize or intensify an action: *Estoy hablando; Estaba hablando.*

§7.5 – 16
Passive Voice

Passive voice means that the action of the verb falls on the subject; in other words, the subject receives the action:

La ventana fue abierta por el ladrón. / The window was opened by the robber.

Note that *abierta* (really a form of the past participle *abrir* / *abierto*) is used as an adjective and it must agree in gender and number with the subject that it describes.

Active voice means that the subject performs the action and the subject is always stated:

El ladrón abrió la ventana. / The robber opened the window.

To form the true passive, use *ser* + the past participle of the verb you have in mind; the past participle then serves as an adjective and it must agree in gender and number with the subject that it describes, as in the example given above. In the true passive, the agent (the doer) is always expressed with the preposition *por* in front of it. The formula for the true passive construction is: subject + tense of *ser* + past participle + *por* + the agent (the doer):

Estas composiciones fueron escritas por Juan. / These compositions were written by John.

The reflexive pronoun *se* may be used to substitute for the true passive voice construction. When you use the *se* construction, the subject is a thing (not a person) and the doer (agent) is not stated:

Aquí se habla español. / Spanish is spoken here.
Aquí se hablan español e inglés. / Spanish and English are spoken here.
Se venden libros en esta tienda. / Books are sold in this store.

There are a few standard idiomatic expressions that are commonly used with the pronoun *se*. These expressions are not truly passive, the pronoun *se* is not truly a reflexive pronoun, and the verb form is in the 3rd person singular only. In this construction, there is no subject expressed; the subject is contained in the use of *se* + the 3rd person singular of the verb at all times and the common translations into English are: it is . . . , people . . . , they . . . , one . . . .

Se cree que . . . / It is believed that . . . , people believe that . . . , they believe that . . . , one believes that . . .

> *Se cree que este criminal es culpable.* / It is believed that
> this criminal is guilty.

Se dice que . . . / It is said that . . . , people say that . . . ,
they say that . . . , one says that . . . , you say . . .

> *Se dice que va a nevar esta noche.* / They say that it's going
> to snow tonight.
> *¿Cómo se dice en español* ice cream? / How do you say
> "ice cream" in Spanish?

Se sabe que . . . / It is known that . . . , people know
that . . . , they know that . . . , one knows that . . .

> *Se sabe que María va a casarse con Juan.* / People know
> that Mary is going to marry John.

The *se* reflexive pronoun construction is avoided if the
subject is a person because there can be ambiguity in
meaning. For example, how would you translate into
English the following: *Se da un regalo.* Which of the following two meanings is intended? She (he) is being given a
present, or She (he) is giving a present to himself (to
herself). In correct Spanish you would have to say: *Le da (a
María, a Juan,* etc.) *un regalo.* / He (she) is giving a present
to Mary (to John, etc.). Avoid using the *se* construction in
the passive when the subject is a person; change your
sentence around and state it in the active voice to make the
meaning clear. Otherwise, the pronoun *se* seems to go with
the verb, as if the verb itself is reflexive, which gives an
entirely different meaning. Another example: *Se miró* would
mean "He (she) looked at himself (herself)," not "He (she)
was looked at!" If you mean to say He (she) looked at him
(at her), say: *La miró* or, if in the plural, say *La miraron.* /
They looked at her.

§7.5 – 17
Imperative OR
Command
Mood

The imperative mood is used in Spanish and in English to
express a command. We saw earlier that the subjunctive
mood is used to express commands in the *Ud.* and *Uds.*
forms, in addition to other uses of the subjunctive mood.

Here are other points you ought to know about the
imperative.

• An indirect command or deep desire expressed in the third
person singular or plural is in the subjunctive. Notice the
use of "Let" or "May" in the English translations. *Que*
introduces this kind of command.

¡Que lo haga Jorge! / Let George do it!
¡Que Dios se lo pague! / May God reward you!
¡Que entre Roberto! / Let Robert enter!
¡Que salgan! / Let them leave!

- In some indirect commands, *que* is omitted. Here, too, the subjunctive is used.

  ¡Viva el presidente! / Long live the president!

- The verb form of the affirmative singular familiar *(tú)* is the same as the 3rd person singular of the present indicative when expressing a command.

  ¡Entra pronto! / Come in quickly!
  ¡Sigue leyendo! / Keep on reading! OR Continue reading!

- There are some exceptions, however. The following verb forms are irregular in the affirmative singular imperative *(tú* form only).

  di (decir)   *sal (salir)*   *val (valer)*
  haz (hacer)   *sé (ser)*   *ve (ir)*
  he (haber)   *ten (tener)*   *ven (venir)*
  pon (poner)

- In the affirmative command, 1st person plural, instead of using the present subjunctive command, *vamos a* (Let's or Let us) + infinitive may be used.

  Vamos a comer. OR *Comamos.* / Let's eat.
  Vamos a cantar. OR *Cantemos.* / Let's sing.

- In the affirmative command, 1st person plural, *vamos* may be used to mean "Let's go:"

  Vamos al cine. / Let's go to the movies.

- However, if in the negative (Let's not go), the present subjunctive of *ir* must be used:

  No vayamos al cine. / Let's not go to the movies.

- Note that *Vámonos* (1st person plural of *irse,* imperative) means "Let's go" or "Let's go away" or "Let's leave."

- Also note that *no nos vayamos* (1st person plural of *irse,* present subjunctive) means "Let's not go" or "Let's not go away" or "Let's not leave."

- The imperative in the affirmative familiar plural *(vosotros, vosotras)* is formed by dropping the final *r* of the infinitive and adding *d.*

  ¡Hablad! / Speak!   *¡Id!* / Go!
  ¡Comed! / Eat!   *¡Venid!* / Come!

- When forming the affirmative familiar plural *(vosotros, vosotras)* imperative of a reflexive verb, the final *d* on the infinitive must be dropped before the reflexive pronoun *os* is added, and both elements are joined to make one word.

  ¡Levantaos! / Get up!   *¡Sentaos!* / Sit down!

- When the final d is dropped in a reflexive verb ending in -ir, an accent mark must be written on the *i*.

  ¡Vestíos! / Get dressed!   *¡Divertíos!* / Have a good time!

- When forming the 1st person plural affirmative imperative of a reflexive verb, the final *s* must drop before the reflexive pronoun *os* is added, and both elements are joined to make one word. This requires an accent mark on the vowel of the syllable that was stressed before *os* was added.
  Vamos + nos changes to:

  ¡Vámonos! / Let's go! or Let's go away! or Let's leave!

- All negative imperatives in the familiar 2nd person singular *(tú)* and plural *(vosotros, vosotras)* are expressed in the present subjunctive.

  ¡No corras (tú)! / Don't run!
  ¡No corráis (vosotros or vosotras)! / Don't run!

- Object pronouns (direct, indirect, or reflexive) with an imperative verb form in the affirmative are attached to the verb form. Examples:

  ¡Hágalo (Ud.)! / Do it!
  ¡Díganoslo (Ud.)! / Tell it to us!
  ¡Dímelo (tú)! / Tell it to me!
  ¡Levántate (tú)! / Get up!

- Object pronouns (direct, indirect, or reflexive) with an imperative verb form in the negative are placed in front of the verb form. Compare the following examples with those given above:

  ¡No lo haga (Ud.)! / Don't do it!
  ¡No nos lo diga (Ud.)! / Don't tell it to us!
  ¡No me lo digas (tú)! / Don't tell it to me!
  ¡No te levantes (tú)! / Don't get up!

- Note that in Latin America the 2nd person plural familiar *(vosotros, vosotras)* forms are avoided. In place of them, the 3rd person plural *Uds.* forms are customarily used.

§7.5–18
Subjunctive

The subjunctive is not a tense; it is a mood or mode. Usually, when we speak in Spanish or English, we use the indicative mood. We use the subjunctive mood in Spanish for certain reasons.

Uses

7.5–18.1 AFTER CERTAIN CONJUNCTIONS

When the following conjunctions introduce a new clause, the verb in that new clause is in the subjunctive mood:

a fin de que / so that, in order that
a menos que / unless
como si / as if
con tal que or *con tal de que* / provided that
para que / in order that, so that
sin que / without

EXAMPLES:
Se lo explico a ustedes a fin de que puedan comprenderlo. / I am explaining it to you so that (in order that) you may be able to understand it.
Saldré a las tres y media a menos que esté lloviendo. / I will go out at three thirty unless it is raining.

When the following conjunctions introduce a new clause, the verb in that new clause is sometimes in the indicative mood, sometimes in the subjunctive mood. Use the subjunctive mood if what is being expressed indicates some sort of anxious anticipation, doubt, indefiniteness, vagueness, or uncertainty. If these are not implied and if the action was completed in the past, use the indicative mood:

a pesar de que / in spite of the fact that
así que / as soon as, after
aunque / although, even if, even though
cuando / when
de manera que / so that, so as
de modo que / so that, in such a way that
después que or *después de que* / after
en cuanto / as soon as
hasta que / until
luego que / as soon as, after
mientras / while, as long as
siempre que / whenever, provided that

EXAMPLES:
Le daré el dinero a Roberto cuando me lo pida. / I shall give the money to Robert when he asks me for it. (*Pida* is in the subjunctive mood because some doubt or uncertainty is suggested and Robert may not ask for it.)

BUT

Se lo di a Roberto cuando me lo pidió. / I gave it to Robert
  when he asked me for it. (No subjunctive of *pedir* here
  because he actually did ask me for it.)
Esperaré hasta que llegue el autobús. / I shall wait until the bus
  arrives. (*Llegue* is in the subjunctive mood here because
  some doubt or uncertainty is suggested and the bus may
  never arrive.)

BUT

Esperé hasta que llegó el autobús. / I waited until the bus
  arrived. (No subjunctive of *llegar* here because the bus
  actually did arrive.)

7.5–18.2 AFTER CERTAIN ADVERBS

acaso *quizá* or *quizás* *tal vez*	perhaps, maybe

Tal vez hayan perdido. / Perhaps they have lost. (Subjunctive is
  used here because some degree of uncertainty or pessimism
  is implied.)
Tal vez han ganado. / Perhaps they have won. (No subjunctive
  is used here because some degree of certainty or optimism
  is implied.)
Por + adjective or adverb + *que* / however, no matter how
Por (más) interesante que sea, no quiero ver esa película. / No
  matter how interesting it may be, I do not want to see that film.

7.5–18.3 AFTER CERTAIN INDEFINITE EXPRESSIONS

cualquier, cualquiera, cualesquier, cualesquiera / whatever,
  whichever, any (the final *a* drops in *cualquiera* and
  cualesquiera when the word is in front of a noun)
cuandoquiera / whenever
dondequiera / wherever; *adondequiera* / to wherever
quienquiera, quienesquiera / whoever

EXAMPLES:
Dondequiera que Ud. esté, escríbame. / Wherever you may be,
  write to me.
Adondequiera que Ud. vaya, dígamelo. / Wherever you may go,
  tell me.

7.5–18.4 AFTER AN INDEFINITE OR NEGATIVE ANTECEDENT

The reason why the subjunctive is needed after an indefinite or negative antecedent is that the person or thing desired may possibly not exist; or, if it does exist, you may never find it.

EXAMPLES:

Busco un libro que sea interesante. / I am looking for a book that is interesting.

BUT

Tengo un libro que es interesante. / I have a book that is interesting.

¿Conoce Ud. a alguien que tenga paciencia? / Do you know someone who has patience?

BUT

Conozco a alguien que tiene paciencia. / I know someone who has patience.

No encontré a nadie que supiera la respuesta. / I did not find anyone who knew the answer.

BUT

Encontré a alguien que sabe la respuesta. / I found someone who knows the answer.

7.5–18.5 AFTER ¡Que . . . !

In order to express indirectly a wish, an order, a command in the 3rd person singular or plural, you may use the exclamatory ¡Que . . . ! alone to introduce the subjunctive clause.

¡Que lo haga Jorge! / Let George do it!
¡Que entre! / Let him enter!

7.5–18.6 AFTER ¡Ojalá que . . . !

The exclamatory expression *Ojalá* is one of Arabic origin meaning "Oh, God!"

¡Ojalá que vengan! / If only they would come!
¡Ojalá que lleguen! / If only they would arrive!

7.5–18.7 AFTER CERTAIN IMPERSONAL EXPRESSIONS

Basta que . . . / It is enough that . . . ; It is sufficient that . . .
Conviene que . . . / It is fitting that . . . ; It is proper that . . .
Importa que . . . / It is important that . . .
Más vale que . . . / It is better that . . .
Es aconsejable que . . . / It is advisable that . . .

EXAMPLES:

Basta que sepan la verdad. / It is sufficient that they know the
   truth.
Conviene que venga ahora mismo. / It is proper that she come
   right now.
Es aconsejable que salga inmediatamente. / It is advisable that
   she leave immediately.

7.5–18.8 AFTER VERBS OR EXPRESSIONS THAT INDICATE DENIAL, DOUBT OR LACK OF BELIEF, AND UNCERTAINTY

---

dudar que . . . / to doubt that . . .
negar que . . . / to deny that . . .
no creer que . . . / not to believe that . . .
Es dudoso que . . . / It is doubtful that . . .
Es incierto que . . . / It is uncertain that . . .
Hay duda que . . . / There is doubt that . . .
No es cierto que . . . / It is not certain that . . .
No estar seguro que . . . / Not to be sure that . . .

EXAMPLES:

Dudo que mis amigos vengan. / I doubt that my friends are
                              coming.
No creo que sea urgente. / I do not believe that it is urgent.

7.5–18.9 AFTER VERBS OR EXPRESSIONS THAT INDICATE AN EMOTION

---

estar contento que . . . / to be happy that . . . , to be
   pleased that . . .
estar feliz que . . . / to be happy that . . .
estar triste que . . . / to be sad that . . .
alegrarse (de) que . . . / to be glad that . . .
sentir que . . . / to regret that . . . , to feel sorry that . . .

EXAMPLES:

Estoy muy contento que mis amigos vengan a verme / I am
   very pleased that my friends are coming (will come) to see me.
Me alegro de que ellos hayan venido / I am glad that they have
   come.

7.5–18.10 AFTER CERTAIN VERBS THAT IMPLY A WISH OR DESIRE THAT SOMETHING BE DONE, INCLUDING A COMMAND, ORDER, PREFERENCE, ADVICE, PERMISSION, REQUEST, PLEA, INSISTENCE, SUGGESTION

aconsejar / to advise
decir / to tell (someone to do something)
desear / to want, to wish
mandar / to order, to command
pedir / to ask, to request
preferir / to prefer
prohibir / to forbid, to prohibit
querer / to want, to wish
rogar / to beg, to request
sugerir / to suggest

EXAMPLES:

Les aconsejo a ellos que hagan el trabajo. / I advise them to do the work.

Les digo a ellos que escriban los ejercicios. / I am telling them to write the exercises.

Mi madre quiere que yo vaya a la escuela. / My mother wants me to go to school.

BUT

Yo quiero ir a la escuela. / I want to go to school.

Note: In this example, there is no change in subject; therefore, the infinitive *ir* is used. But in the example above, beginning with *Mi madre quiere que . . . ,* there is a new subject *(yo)* in the dependent clause and *ir* is in the subjunctive because the verb *querer* is used in the main clause.

El capitán me manda que yo entre / The captain orders me to come in.

7.5–18.11 SEQUENCE OF TENSES WHEN THE SUBJUNCTIVE IS REQUIRED: A SUMMARY

When the verb in the main clause is in the:	The verb in the following clause (the dependent clause) most likely will be in the:
Present Indicative or Future or Present Perfect Indicative or Imperative (Command)	Present Subjunctive or Present Perfect Subjunctive

Conditional or a past tense (Imperfect Indicative or Preterit or Pluperfect Indicative)	Imperfect Subjunctive or Pluperfect Subjunctive

EXAMPLES:
Deseo que Ana cante. / I want Anna to sing.
Le diré a Ana que baile. / I will tell Anna to dance.
Le he dicho a Ana que cante y baile. / I have said to Anna to sing and dance.
Dígale a Ana que cante y baile. / Tell Anna to sing and dance.
Dudo que mi madre tome el tren. / I doubt that my mother is taking the train.

§7.5 – 19
The Names of Tenses and Moods

The Simple Tenses	The Compound Tenses
Present indicative	Present perfect indicative
Imperfect indicative	Pluperfect OR Past perfect indicative
Preterit	Past anterior OR Preterit perfect
Future	Future perfect OR Future anterior
Conditional	Conditional perfect
Present subjunctive	Present perfect OR Past subjunctive
Imperfect subjunctive	Pluperfect OR Past perfect subjunctive
Imperative OR Command	

Haber (helping verb) in the 7 simple tenses

Present participle: *habiendo*
Past participle: *habido*
Infinitive: *haber*

Present indicative	*he, has, ha; hemos, habéis, han* I have, you have, you or he or she or it has; we have, you have, you or they have
Imperfect indicative	*había, habías, había; habíamos, habíais, habían* I had, you had, you or he or she or it had; we had, you had, you or they had
Preterit	*hube, hubiste, hubo; hubimos, hubisteis, hubieron* I had, you had, you or he or she or it had; we had, you had, you or they had

Haber (helping verb) in the 7 simple tenses

Present participle: *habiendo*
Past participle: *habido*
Infinitive: *haber*

Future	*habré, habrás, habrá; habremos, habréis, habrán* I shall have, you will have, you or he or she or it will have; we shall have, you will have, you or they will have
Conditional	*habría, habrías, habría; habríamos, habríais, habrían* I would have, you would have, you or he or she or it would have; we would have, you would have, you or they would have
Present subjunctive	*haya, hayas, haya; hayamos, hayáis, hayan* that I may have, that you may have, that you or he or she or it may have; that we may have, that you may have, that you or they may have
Imperfect subjunctive	(the *-ra* form): *hubiera, hubieras, hubiera; hubiéramos, hubierais, hubieran* OR (the *-se* form): *hubiese, hubieses, hubiese; hubiésemos, hubieseis, hubiesen* that I might have, that you might have, that you or he or she or it might have; that we might have, that you might have, that you or they might have

Note: The subject pronouns in Spanish were omitted above in order to emphasize the verb forms.

Singular: *yo, tú, Ud.* OR *él* OR *ella;*
Plural: *nosotros (nosotras), vosotros (vosotras), Uds.* OR *ellos* OR *ellas*

§7.6
SPECIAL CASES
AND VERBS
WITH SPECIAL
MEANINGS

§7.6 – 1
Si Clause: A
Summary of
Contrary-to-
Fact
Conditions

When the verb in the *Si* clause is:	The verb in the main or result clause is:
Present Indicative	Future

EXAMPLE:
Si tengo bastante tiempo, vendré a verle. / If I have enough
   time, I will come to see you.

Note that the present subjunctive form of a verb is
never used in a clause beginning with the conjunction *si*.

Imperfect Subjunctive (-*se* form or -*ra* form)	Conditional or Imperfect Subjunctive (-*ra* form)

EXAMPLE:
Si yo tuviese (or *tuviera*) *bastante tiempo, vendría a verle.* / If
   I had enough time, I would come to see you.

OR

Si yo tuviese (or *tuviera*) *bastante tiempo, viniera a verle.* / If
   I had enough time, I would come to see you.

Pluperfect Subjunctive (-*se* form or -*ra* form)	Conditional Perfect or Pluperfect Subjunctive (-*ra* form)

EXAMPLE:
Si yo hubiese tenido (or *hubiera tenido*) *bastante tiempo,*
habría venido a verle. / If I had had enough time, I would
   have come to see you.

OR

Si yo hubiese tenido (or *hubiera tenido*) *bastante tiempo,*
hubiera venido a verle. / If I had had enough time, I would
   have come to see you.

§7.6 – 2
Acabar de +
Infinitive

In the present indicative:

   María acaba de llegar. / Mary has just arrived.
   Acabo de comer. / I have just eaten.
   Acabamos de terminar la lección. / We have just finished the
     lesson.

When you use *acabar* in the present tense, it indicates that the action of the main verb (+ infinitive) has just occurred now in the present. In English, we express this by using have just + the past participle of the main verb.

In the imperfect indicative:

María acababa de llegar. / Mary had just arrived.
Acababa de comer. / I had just eaten.
Acabábamos de terminar la lección. / We had just finished the lesson.

When you use *acabar* in the imperfect indicative, it indicates that the action of the main verb (+ infinitive) had occurred at some time in the past when another action occurred. In English, we express this by using had just + the past participle of the main verb.

§7.6–3 Conocer and saber

These two verbs mean to know, but they are used differently.

• *Conocer* means to know in the sense of being acquainted with a person, a place, or a thing:

¿Conoce Ud. a María? / Do you know Mary?
¿Conoce Ud. bien los Estados Unidos? / Do you know the United States well?
¿Conoce Ud. este libro? / Do you know (Are you acquainted with) this book?

In the preterit tense, *conocer* means met in the sense of first met, first became acquainted with someone:

¿Conoce Ud. a Elena? / Do you know Helen?
Sí, (yo) la conocí anoche en casa de un amigo mío. / Yes, I met her [for the first time] last night at the home of one of my friends.

• *Saber* means to know a fact, to know something thoroughly:

¿Sabe Ud. qué hora es? / Do you know what time it is?

When you use *saber* + infinitive, it means to know how:

¿Sabe Ud. nadar? / Do you know how to swim?
Sí, (yo) sé nadar. / Yes, I know how to swim.

In the preterit tense, *saber* means found out:

¿Lo sabe Ud.? / Do you know it?
Sí, lo supe ayer. / Yes, I found it out yesterday.

§7.6 – 4
Deber, deber de and *tener que*

Generally speaking, use *deber* when you want to express a moral obligation, something you ought to do but you may or may not do it:

Debo estudiar esta noche pero estoy cansado y no me siento bien. / I ought to study tonight but I am tired and I do not feel well.

Generally speaking, *deber de* + infinitive is used to express a supposition, something that is probable:

La señora Gómez debe de estar enferma porque sale de casa raramente. / Mrs. Gómez must be sick (is probably sick) because she goes out of the house rarely.

Generally speaking, use *tener que* when you want to say that you have to do something:

No puedo salir esta noche porque tengo que estudiar. / I cannot go out tonight because I have to study.

§7.6 – 5
Dejar, salir and *salir de*

These verbs mean to leave, but notice the uses:
   Use *dejar* when you leave someone or when you leave something behind you:

El alumno dejó sus libros en la sala de clase. / The pupil left his books in the classroom.

Dejar also means to let or to allow or to let go:

Déjelo! / Let it! (Leave it!)

   Use *salir de* when you mean to leave in the sense of to go out of (a place):

El alumno salió de la sala de clase. / The pupil left the classroom.
¿Dónde está su madre? Mi madre salió. / Where is your mother? My mother went out.

§7.6 – 6
Dejar de + Infinitive and *dejar caer*

Use *dejar de* + infinitive when you mean to stop or to fail to:

Los alumnos dejaron de hablar. / The students stopped talking.
¡No deje Ud. de llamarme! / Don't fail to call me!

Dejar caer means to drop:

Luis dejó caer sus libros. / Louis dropped his books.

§7.6–7
Ir, irse

Use *ir* when you simply mean to go:

Voy al cine. / I am going to the movies.

Use *irse* when you mean to leave in the sense of to go away:

Mis padres se fueron al campo para visitar a mis abuelos. / My parents left for (went away to) the country to visit my grandparents.

§7.6–8
Gastar and *pasar*

These two verbs mean to spend, but notice the uses:
Use *gastar* when you spend money:

No me gusta gastar mucho dinero. / I don't like to spend much money.

Use *pasar* when you spend time:

Me gustaría pasar un año en España. / I would like to spend a year in Spain.

§7.6–9
Gustar

- Essentially, the verb *gustar* means to be pleasing to . . .
- In English, we say, for example, I like ice cream. In Spanish, we say *Me gusta el helado.*
- In English, the thing that you like is the direct object. In Spanish, the thing that you like is the subject. Also, in Spanish, the person who likes the thing is the indirect object: to me, to you, etc.:

  A Roberto le gusta el helado. / Robert likes ice cream; in other words, "To Robert, ice cream is pleasing to him."

- In Spanish, therefore, the verb *gustar* is used in the third person, either in the singular or plural, when you talk about something that you like—something that is pleasing to you. Therefore, the verb form must agree with the subject; if the thing liked is singular, the verb is third person singular; if the thing liked is plural, the verb *gustar* is third person plural:

  Me gusta el café. / I like coffee.
  Me gustan el café y la leche. / I like coffee and milk.

- When you mention the person or the persons who like something, you must use the preposition *a* in front of the person; you must also use the indirect object pronoun of the noun which is the person:

  A los muchachos y a las muchachas les gusta jugar. / Boys and girls like to play; that is to say, "To play is pleasing to them, to boys and girls."

- Review the indirect object pronouns, which are *me, te, le; nos, os, les.*

EXAMPLES:

Me gusta leer. / I like to read.
Te gusta leer. / You (familiar) like to read.
A Felipe le gusta el helado. / Philip likes ice cream.
Al chico le gusta la leche. / The boy likes milk.
A Carlota le gusta bailar. / Charlotte likes to dance.
A las chicas les gustó el libro. / The girls liked the book.
Nos gustó el cuento. / We liked the story.

§7.6 – 10
Haber, haber de + Infinitive and *tener*

The verb *haber* (to have) is used as an auxiliary verb (or helping verb) in order to form the seven compound tenses.

The verb *haber* is also used to form the perfect (or past) infinitive: *haber hablado* (to have spoken). This is formed by using the infinitive form of *haber* + the past participle of the main verb.

The verb *haber* is also used to form the perfect participle: *habiendo hablado* (having spoken). This is formed by using the present participle of *haber* + the past participle of the main verb.

The verb *haber* + *de* + infinitive is equivalent to the English use of "to be supposed to . . ." or "to be to . . .".

EXAMPLE:

María ha de traer un pastel, yo he de traer el helado, y mis amigos han de traer sus discos. / Mary is supposed to bring a pie, I am supposed to bring the ice cream, and my friends are to bring their records.

The verb *tener* is used to mean to have in the sense of to possess or to hold:

Tengo un perro y un gato. / I have a dog and a cat.

In the preterit tense, *tener* can mean received:

Ayer mi padre tuvo un cheque. / Yesterday my father received a check.

§7.6 – 11
Jugar and *tocar*

Both these verbs mean to play but they have different uses. *Jugar a* is used to play a sport, a game:

¿Juega Ud. al tenis? / Do you play tennis?
Me gusta jugar a la pelota. / I like to play ball.

The verb *tocar* is used to play a musical instrument:

Carmen toca muy bien el piano. / Carmen plays the piano very well.

The verb *tocar* has other meanings: to be one's turn, in which case it takes an indirect object:

¿A quién le toca? / Whose turn is it?
Le toca a Juan. / It is John's turn.

to knock on a door:

tocar a la puerta; Alguien toca a la puerta. / Someone is knocking on (at) the door.

Essentially, *tocar* means to touch.

§7.6 – 12
Llegar a ser, hacerse and *ponerse*

These three verbs mean to become. Note the uses:
Use *llegar a ser* + a noun: to become a doctor, to become a teacher; in other words, the noun indicates the goal that you are striving for:

Quiero llegar a ser doctor. / I want to become a doctor.

Hacerse is used similarly:

Juan se hizo abogado. / John became a lawyer.

Use *ponerse* + an adjective: to become pale, to become sick; in other words, the adjective indicates the state or condition (physical or mental) that you have become:

Cuando vi el accidente, me puse pálido. / When I saw the accident, I became pale.
Mi madre se puso triste al oír la noticia desgraciada. / My mother became sad upon hearing the unfortunate news.

§7.6 – 13
Llevar and *tomar*

These two verbs mean to take but note the uses:
Llevar means to take in the sense of carry or transport from place to place:

José llevó la silla de la cocina al comedor. / Joseph took the chair from the kitchen to the dining room.

The verb *llevar* is also used when you take someone somewhere:

Pedro llevó a María al baile anoche. / Peter took Mary to the dance last night.

As you probably know, *llevar* also means to wear:

María, ¿por qué llevas la falda nueva? / Mary, why are you wearing your new skirt?

Tomar means to take in the sense of grab or catch:

La profesora tomó el libro y comenzó a leer a la clase. / The teacher took the book and began to read to the class.
Mi amigo tomó el tren esta mañana a las siete. / My friend took the train this morning at seven o'clock.

§7.6 – 14
Pedir and *preguntar*

Both these verbs mean to ask but note the uses:
Pedir means to ask for something or to request:

El alumno pidió un lápiz al profesor. / The pupil asked the teacher for a pencil.

Preguntar means to inquire, to ask a question:

La alumna preguntó a la profesora cómo estaba. / The pupil asked the teacher how she was.

§7.6 – 15
Pensar de and *pensar en*

Both these verbs mean to think of but note the uses:
Pensar is used with the preposition *de* when you ask someone what he/she thinks of someone or something, when you ask for someone's opinion:

¿Qué piensa Ud. de este libro? / What do you think of this book?
Pienso que es bueno. / I think that it is good.

Pensar is used with the preposition *en* when you ask someone what or whom he/she is thinking about:

Miguel, no hablas mucho; ¿en qué piensas? / Michael, you are not talking much; of what are you thinking? (what are you thinking of?)
Pienso en las vacaciones de verano. / I'm thinking of summer vacation.

§7.6 – 16
Poder and *saber*

Both these verbs mean can, but note the uses:
Poder means can in the sense of ability:

No puedo ayudarle; lo siento. / I cannot (am unable to) help you; I'm sorry.

Saber means can in the sense of to know how:

Este niño no sabe contar. / This child can't (does not know how to) count.

In the preterit tense, *poder* has the special meaning of succeeded:

Después de algunos minutos, Juan pudo abrir la puerta. / After a few minutes, John succeeded in opening the door.

In the preterit tense, *saber* has the special meaning of found out:

Lo supe ayer. / I found it out yesterday.

§7.6 – 17
Ser and estar

These two verbs mean to be but note the uses:

Generally speaking, use *ser* when you want to express to be.

Use *estar* when to be is used in the following ways:

Health:

¿Cómo está Ud.? / How are you?
Estoy bien. / I am well.
Estoy enfermo (enferma). / I am sick.

Location: persons, places, things:

Estoy en la sala de clase. / I am in the classroom.
La escuela está lejos. / The school is far.
Barcelona está en España. / Barcelona is (located) in Spain.

State or condition: persons

Estoy contento (contenta). / I am happy.
Los alumnos están cansados. (Las alumnas están cansadas). / The students are tired.
María está triste hoy. / Mary is sad today.
Estoy listo (lista). / I am ready.
Estoy pálido (pálida). / I am pale.
Estoy ocupado (ocupada). / I am busy.

State or condition: things and places

La ventana está abierta. / The window is open.
La taza está llena. / The cup is full.
El té está caliente. / The tea is hot.

To form the progressive present of a verb, use the present tense of *estar* + the present participle of the main verb.

Estoy estudiando en mi cuarto y no puedo salir esta noche. / I am studying in my room and I cannot go out tonight.

To form the progressive past of a verb, use the imperfect tense of *estar* + the present participle of the main verb.

Mi hermano estaba leyendo cuando (yo) entré en el cuarto. / My brother was reading when I entered (came into) the room.

§7.6 – 18
Volver and devolver

These two verbs mean to return but note the uses:

Volver means to return in the sense of to come back:

Voy a volver a casa. / I am going to return home.

A synonym of *volver* is *regresar:*

Los muchachos regresaron a las ocho de la noche. / The boys came back at eight o'clock in the evening.

Devolver means to return in the sense of to give back:

Voy a devolver el libro a la biblioteca. / I am going to return the book to the library.

§7.7 COMMONLY USED BASIC IRREGULAR VERBS

§7.7–1 Present Indicative

acordarse / to remember
me acuerdo,
te acuerdas, se acuerda;
nos acordamos,
os acordáis, se acuerdan

acostarse / to go to bed, to lie down
me acuesto, te acuestas,
se acuesta;
nos acostamos,
os acostáis, se acuestan

almorzar / to lunch, to have lunch
almuerzo, almuerzas,
almuerza; almorzamos,
almorzáis, almuerzan

aparecer / to appear, to show up
aparezco, apareces,
aparece; aparecemos,
aparecéis, aparecen

caber / to fit, to be contained
quepo, cabes, cabe;
cabemos, cabéis, caben

caer / to fall
caigo, caes, cae;
caemos, caéis, caen

cerrar / to close
cierro, cierras, cierra;
cerramos, cerráis, cierran

cocer / to cook
cuezo, cueces, cuece;
cocemos, cocéis, cuecen

coger / to seize, to grasp, to grab, to catch
cojo, coges, coge;
cogemos, cogéis, cogen

comenzar / to begin, to start, to commence
comienzo, comienzas,
comienza; comenzamos,
comenzáis, comienzan

conducir / to conduct, to lead, to drive
conduzco, conduces,
conduce; conducimos,
conducís, conducen

conocer / to know, to be acquainted with
conozco, conoces,
conoce; conocemos,
conocéis, conocen

contar / to count, to relate
cuento, cuentas, cuenta;
contamos, contáis,
cuentan

corregir / to correct
corrijo, corriges, corrige;
corregimos, corregís,
corrigen

costar / to cost
cuesta; cuestan

dar / to give
doy, das, da; damos,
dais, dan

decir / to say, to tell
digo, dices, dice;
decimos, decís, dicen

despertarse / to awaken,
to wake up (oneself)
me despierto,
te despiertas,
se despierta;
nos despertamos,
os despertáis,
se despiertan

devolver / to return, to give
back (something)
devuelvo, devuelves,
devuelve; devolvemos,
devolvéis, devuelven

divertirse / to have a good
time, to enjoy oneself
me divierto, te diviertes,
se divierte;
nos divertimos,
os divertís, se divierten

doler / to ache, to pain, to
hurt, to cause grief, to
cause regret
duelo, dueles, duele;
dolemos, doléis, duelen

dormir / to sleep
duermo, duermes,
duerme; dormimos,
dormís, duermen

dormirse / to fall asleep
me duermo, te duermes,
se duerme;
nos dormimos,
os dormís, se duermen

empezar / to begin, to start
empiezo, empiezas,
empieza; empezamos,
empezáis, empiezan

encontrar / to meet, to
encounter, to find
encuentro, encuentras,
encuentra; encontramos,
encontráis, encuentran

entender / to understand
entiendo, entiendes,
entiende; entendemos,
entendéis, entienden

enviar / to send
envío, envías, envía;
enviamos, enviáis, envían

estar / to be
estoy, estás, está;
estamos, estáis, están

haber / to have (as an
auxiliary or helping verb)
he, has, ha; hemos,
habéis, han

hacer / to do, to make
hago, haces, hace;
hacemos, hacéis, hacen

helar / to freeze
hiela OR está helando (in
the present progressive
form)

ir / to go
voy, vas, va; vamos,
vais, van

irse / to go away
me voy, te vas, se va;
nos vamos, os vais,
se van

jugar / to play
juego, juegas, juega;
jugamos, jugáis, juegan

llover / to rain
llueve OR está lloviendo
(in the present
progressive form)

morir / to die
muero, mueres, muere;
morimos, morís, mueren

mostrar / to show, to point
out
muestro, muestras,
muestra; mostramos,
mostráis, muestran

nacer / to be born
nazco, naces, nace;
nacemos, nacéis, nacen

nevar / to snow
nieva OR está nevando
(in the present
progressive form)

obtener / to obtain, to get
obtengo, obtienes,
obtiene; obtenemos,
obtenéis, obtienen

oír / to hear
oigo, oyes, oye; oímos,
oís, oyen

pedir / to ask for, to request
pido, pides, pide;
pedimos, pedís, piden

pensar / to think
pienso, piensas, piensa;
pensamos, pensáis,
piensan

perder / to lose
pierdo, pierdes, pierde;
perdemos, perdéis,
pierden

poder / to be able, can
puedo, puedes, puede;
podemos, podéis, pueden

poner / to put, to place
pongo, pones, pone;
ponemos, ponéis, ponen

querer / to want, to wish
quiero, quieres, quiere;
queremos, queréis,
quieren

recordar / to remember
recuerdo, recuerdas,
recuerda; recordamos,
recordáis, recuerdan

reír / to laugh
río, ríes, ríe; reímos, reís,
ríen

repetir / to repeat
repito, repites, repite;
repetimos, repetís,
repiten

saber / to know, to know
how
sé, sabes, sabe;
sabemos, sabéis, saben

salir / to go out
salgo, sales, sale;
salimos, salís, salen

seguir / to follow, to
pursue, to continue
sigo, sigues, sigue;
seguimos, seguís, siguen

sentarse / to sit down
me siento, te sientas,
se sienta; nos sentamos,
os sentáis, se sientan

sentir / to feel sorry, to
regret, to feel, to
experience, to sense
siento, sientes, siente;
sentimos, sentís, sienten

sentirse / to feel (well, sick)
me siento, te sientes,
se siente; nos sentimos,
os sentís, se sienten

ser / to be
soy, eres, es; somos,
sois, son

servir / to serve
sirvo, sirves, sirve;
servimos, servís, sirven

soñar / to dream
sueño, sueñas, sueña;
soñamos, soñáis, sueñan

sonreír / to smile
sonrío, sonríes, sonríe;
sonreímos, sonreís,
sonríen

tener / to have, to hold
tengo, tienes, tiene;
tenemos, tenéis, tienen

traer / to bring
traigo, traes, trae;
traemos, traéis, traen

venir / to come
vengo, vienes, viene;
venimos, venís, vienen

ver / to see
veo, ves, ve; vemos,
veis, ven

volver / to return
vuelvo, vuelves, vuelve;
volvemos, volvéis, vuelven

§7.7–2 Imperfect Indicative

ir / to go (I was going, I
used to go, etc.)
iba, ibas, iba; íbamos,
ibais, iban

ser / to be (I was, I used to
be, etc.)
era, eras, era; éramos,
erais, eran

ver / to see (I was seeing, I
used to see, etc.)
veía, veías, veía;
veíamos, veíais, veían

§7.7–3 Preterit

acercarse / to approach, to
draw near
me acerqué,
te acercaste, se acercó;
nos acercamos,
os acercasteis,
se acercaron

almorzar / to have lunch, to
eat lunch
almorcé, almorzaste,
almorzó; almorzamos,
almorzasteis, almorzaron

andar / to walk
anduve, anduviste,
anduvo; anduvimos,
anduvisteis, anduvieron

buscar / to look for, to
search, to seek
busqué, buscaste,
buscó; buscamos,
buscasteis, buscaron

caber / to fit, to be
contained
cupe, cupiste, cupo;
cupimos, cupisteis,
cupieron

caer / to fall
caí, caíste, cayó; caímos,
caísteis, cayeron

comenzar / to begin, to
commence, to start
comencé, comenzaste,
comenzó; comenzamos,
comenzasteis,
comenzaron

conducir / to conduct, to
lead, to drive
conduje, condujiste,
condujo; condujimos,
condujisteis, condujeron

creer / to believe
creí, creíste, creyó;
creímos, creísteis,
creyeron

dar / to give
di, diste, dio; dimos,
disteis, dieron

decir / to say, to tell
dije, dijiste, dijo; dijimos,
dijisteis, dijeron

detener / to detain, to stop
(someone or something)
detuve, detuviste,
detuvo; detuvimos,
detuvisteis, detuvieron

detenerse / to stop (oneself
  or itself)
  me detuve, te detuviste,
  se detuvo; nos detuvimos,
  os detuvisteis, se detuvieron
estar / to be
  estuve, estuviste,
  estuvo; estuvimos,
  estuvisteis, estuvieron
haber / to have (as an
  auxiliary or helping verb)
  hube, hubiste, hubo;
  hubimos, hubisteis,
  hubieron
hacer / to do, to make
  hice, hiciste, hizo;
  hicimos, hicisteis, hicieron
ir / to go
  fui, fuiste, fue; fuimos,
  fuisteis, fueron
irse / to go away
  me fui, te fuiste, se fue;
  nos fuimos, os fuisteis,
  se fueron
leer / to read
  leí, leíste, leyó; leímos,
  leísteis, leyeron
llegar / to arrive
  llegué, llegaste, llegó;
  llegamos, llegasteis, llegaron
oír / to hear (sometimes
  can mean "to understand")
  oí, oíste, oyó; oímos,
  oísteis, oyeron
poder / to be able, can
  pude, pudiste, pudo;
  pudimos, pudisteis, pudieron

poner / to put, to place
  puse, pusiste, puso;
  pusimos, pusisteis,
  pusieron
querer / to want, to wish
  quise, quisiste, quiso;
  quisimos, quisisteis,
  quisieron
reír / to laugh
  reí, reíste, rió; reímos,
  reísteis, rieron
saber / to know, to know
  how
  supe, supiste, supo;
  supimos, supisteis,
  supieron
ser / to be
  fui, fuiste, fue; fuimos,
  fuisteis, fueron
  Note that these forms
  are the same for ir in the
  preterit.
tener / to have, to hold
  tuve, tuviste, tuvo;
  tuvimos, tuvisteis,
  tuvieron
traer / to bring
  traje, trajiste, trajo;
  trajimos, trajisteis,
  trajeron
venir / to come
  vine, viniste, vino;
  vinimos, vinisteis, vinieron
ver / to see
  vi, viste, vio; vimos,
  visteis, vieron

§7.7–4
Future

caber / to fit, to be
  contained
  cabré, cabrás, cabrá;
  cabremos, cabréis,
  cabrán
decir / to say, to tell
  diré, dirás, dirá; diremos,
  diréis, dirán

haber / to have (as an
  auxiliary or helping verb)
  habré, habrás, habrá;
  habremos, habréis,
  habrán
hacer / to do, to make
  haré, harás, hará;
  haremos, haréis, harán

poder / to be able, can
podré, podrás, podrá;
podremos, podréis,
podrán

poner / to put, to place
pondré, pondrás,
pondrá; pondremos,
pondréis, pondrán

querer / to want, to wish
querré, querrás, querrá;
querremos, querréis,
querrán

saber / to know, to know
how
sabré, sabrás, sabrá;
sabremos, sabréis,
sabrán

salir / to go out
saldré, saldrás, saldrá;
saldremos, saldréis,
saldrán

tener / to have, to hold
tendré, tendrás, tendrá;
tendremos, tendréis,
tendrán

valer / to be worth, to be
worthy
valdré, valdrás, valdrá;
valdremos, valdréis,
valdrán

venir / to come
vendré, vendrás, vendrá;
vendremos, vendréis,
vendrán

§7.7–5
Conditional

caber / to fit, to be
contained
cabría, cabrías, cabría;
cabríamos, cabríais,
cabrían

decir / to say, to tell
diría, dirías, diría;
diríamos, diríais, dirían

haber / to have (as an
auxiliary or helping verb)
habría, habrías, habría;
habríamos, habríais,
habrían

hacer / to do, to make
haría, harías, haría;
haríamos, haríais, harían

poder / to be able, can
podría, podrías, podría;
podríamos, podríais,
podrían

poner / to put, to place
pondría, pondrías,
pondría; pondríamos,
pondríais, pondrían

querer / to want, to wish
querría, querrías, querría;
querríamos, querríais,
querrían

saber / to know, to know how
sabría, sabrías, sabría;
sabríamos, sabríais,
sabrían

salir / to go out
saldría, saldrías, saldría;
saldríamos, saldríais,
saldrían

tener / to have, to hold
tendría, tendrías, tendría;
tendríamos, tendríais,
tendrían

valer / to be worth, to be
worthy
valdría, valdrías, valdría;
valdríamos, valdríais,
valdrían

venir / to come
vendría, vendrías,
vendría; vendríamos,
vendríais, vendrían

§7.7–6 Present Subjunctive

dar / to give
dé, des, dé; demos, deis, den

estar / to be
esté, estés, esté; estemos, estéis, estén

haber / to have (as an auxiliary or helping verb)
haya, hayas, haya; hayamos, hayáis, hayan

ir / to go
vaya, vayas, vaya; vayamos, vayáis, vayan

saber / to know, to know how
sepa, sepas, sepa; sepamos, sepáis, sepan

ser / to be
sea, seas, sea; seamos, seáis, sean

§7.7–7 Imperfect Subjunctive

beber / to drink
bebiera, bebieras, bebiera; bebiéramos, bebierais, bebieran
OR
bebiese, bebieses, bebiese; bebiésemos, bebieseis, bebiesen

dar / to give
diera, dieras, diera; diéramos, dierais, dieran
OR
diese, dieses, diese; diésemos, dieseis, diesen

hablar / to speak
hablara, hablaras, hablara; habláramos, hablarais, hablaran
OR
hablase, hablases, hablase; hablásemos, hablaseis, hablasen

leer / to read
leyera, leyeras, leyera; leyéramos, leyerais, leyeran
OR
leyese, leyeses, leyese; leyésemos, leyeseis, leyesen

recibir / to receive
recibiera, recibieras, recibiera; recibiéramos, recibierais, recibieran
OR
recibiese, recibieses, recibiese; recibiésemos, recibieseis, recibiesen

tener / to have
tuviera, tuvieras, tuviera; tuviéramos, tuvierais, tuvieran
OR
tuviese, tuvieses, tuviese; tuviésemos, tuvieseis, tuviesen

§7.7–8 Complete Conjugations

Here are four commonly used irregular verbs conjugated fully in all the tenses and moods.

In the format of the verbs that follow, the subject pronouns have been omitted in order to emphasize the verb forms. The subject pronouns are:

Singular	Plural
yo	nosotros (nosotras)
tú	vosotros (vosotras)
Ud. (él, ella)	Uds. (ellos, ellas)

estar / to be

Present Participle: *estando*   Past Participle: *estado*

THE SEVEN SIMPLE TENSES		THE SEVEN COMPOUND TENSES	
Singular	**Plural**	**Singular**	**Plural**
Present Indicative		Present Perfect Indicative	
estoy	estamos	he estado	hemos estado
estás	estáis	has estado	habéis estado
está	están	ha estado	han estado
Imperfect Indicative		Pluperfect OR Past Perfect Indicative	
estaba	estábamos	había estado	habíamos estado
estabas	estabais	habías estado	habíais estado
estaba	estaban	había estado	habían estado
Preterit		Past Anterior OR Preterit Perfect	
estuve	estuvimos	hube estado	hubimos estado
estuviste	estuvisteis	hubiste estado	hubisteis estado
estuvo	estuvieron	hubo estado	hubieron estado
Future		Future Perfect OR Future Anterior	
estaré	estaremos	habré estado	habremos estado
estarás	estaréis	habrás estado	habréis estado
estará	estarán	habrá estado	habrán estado
Conditional		Conditional Perfect	
estaría	estaríamos	habría estado	habríamos estado
estarías	estaríais	habrías estado	habríais estado
estaría	estarían	habría estado	habrían estado
Present Subjunctive		Present Perfect OR Past Subjunctive	
esté	estemos	haya estado	hayamos estado
estés	estéis	hayas estado	hayáis estado
esté	estén	haya estado	hayan estado
Imperfect Subjunctive		Pluperfect OR Past Perfect Subjunctive	
estuviera	estuviéramos	hubiera estado	hubiéramos estado
estuvieras	estuvierais	hubieras estado	hubierais estado
estuviera	estuvieran	hubiera estado	hubieran estado
OR		OR	
estuviese	estuviésemos	hubiese estado	hubiésemos estado
estuvieses	estuvieseis	hubieses estado	hubieseis estado
estuviese	estuviesen	hubiese estado	hubiesen estado

Imperative

—	estemos
está; no estés	estad; no estéis
esté	estén

Common Idiomatic Expressions Using this Verb

¿Cómo está Ud.?
Estoy muy bien, gracias. ¿Y usted?
Estoy enfermo hoy.

estar para + infinitive / to be about + infinitive
  Estoy para salir. / I am about to go out.
estar por / to be in favor of

hacer / to do, to make

Present Participle: *haciendo*   Past Participle: *hecho*

THE SEVEN SIMPLE TENSES		THE SEVEN COMPOUND TENSES	
Singular	**Plural**	**Singular**	**Plural**
Present Indicative		Present Perfect Indicative	
hago	hacemos	he hecho	hemos hecho
haces	hacéis	has hecho	habéis hecho
hace	hacen	ha hecho	han hecho
Imperfect Indicative		Pluperfect OR Past Perfect Indicative	
hacía	hacíamos	había hecho	habíamos hecho
hacías	hacíais	habías hecho	habíais hecho
hacía	hacían	había hecho	habían hecho
Preterit		Past Anterior OR Preterit Perfect	
hice	hicimos	hube hecho	hubimos hecho
hiciste	hicisteis	hubiste hecho	hubisteis hecho
hizo	hicieron	hubo hecho	hubieron hecho
Future		Future Perfect OR Future Anterior	
haré	haremos	habré hecho	habremos hecho
harás	haréis	habrás hecho	habréis hecho
hará	harán	habrá hecho	habrán hecho
Conditional		Conditional Perfect	
haría	haríamos	habría hecho	habríamos hecho
harías	haríais	habrías hecho	habríais hecho
haría	harían	habría hecho	habrían hecho
Present Subjunctive		Present Perfect OR Past Subjunctive	
haga	hagamos	haya hecho	hayamos hecho
hagas	hagáis	hayas hecho	hayáis hecho
haga	hagan	haya hecho	hayan hecho
Imperfect Subjunctive		Pluperfect OR Past Perfect Subjunctive	
hiciera	hiciéramos	hubiera hecho	hubiéramos hecho
hicieras	hicierais	hubieras hecho	hubierais hecho
hiciera	hicieran	hubiera hecho	hubieran hecho
OR		OR	
hiciese	hiciésemos	hubiese hecho	hubiésemos hecho
hicieses	hicieseis	hubieses hecho	hubieseis hecho
hiciese	hiciesen	hubiese hecho	hubiesen hecho

Imperative	
—	hagamos
haz; no hagas	haced; no hagáis
haga	hagan

Common Idiomatic Expressions Using this Verb

Dicho y hecho. / No sooner said than done.

La práctica hace maestro al novicio. / Practice makes perfect.

ir / to go

Present Participle: *yendo* Past Participle: *ido*

THE SEVEN SIMPLE TENSES		THE SEVEN COMPOUND TENSES	
Singular	**Plural**	**Singular**	**Plural**
Present Indicative		Present Perfect Indicative	
voy	vamos	he ido	hemos ido
vas	vais	has ido	habéis ido
va	van	ha ido	han ido
Imperfect Indicative		Pluperfect OR Past Perfect Indicative	
iba	íbamos	había ido	habíamos ido
ibas	ibais	habías ido	habíais ido
iba	iban	había ido	habían ido
Preterit		Past Anterior OR Preterit Perfect	
fui	fuimos	hube ido	hubimos ido
fuiste	fuisteis	hubiste ido	hubisteis ido
fue	fueron	hubo ido	hubieron ido
Future		Future Perfect OR Future Anterior	
iré	iremos	habré ido	habremos ido
irás	iréis	habrás ido	habréis ido
irá	irán	habrá ido	habrán ido
Conditional		Conditional Perfect	
iría	iríamos	habría ido	habríamos ido
irías	iríais	habrías ido	habríais ido
iría	irían	habría ido	habrían ido
Present Subjunctive		Present Perfect OR Past Subjunctive	
vaya	vayamos	haya ido	hayamos ido
vayas	vayáis	hayas ido	hayáis ido
vaya	vayan	haya ido	hayan ido
Imperfect Subjunctive		Pluperfect OR Past Perfect Subjunctive	
fuera	fuéramos	hubiera ido	hubiéramos ido
fueras	fuerais	hubieras ido	hubierais ido
fuera	fueran	hubiera ido	hubieran ido
OR		OR	
fuese	fuésemos	hubiese ido	hubiésemos ido
fueses	fueseis	hubieses ido	hubieseis ido
fuese	fuesen	hubiese ido	hubiesen ido

Imperative

	—	vamos (no vayamos)
	ve; no vayas	id; no vayáis
	vaya	vayan

Common Idiomatic Expressions Using this Verb

ir de compras / to go shopping *ir a caballo* / to ride horseback *un billete de ida y vuelta* / round trip ticket

ir de brazo / to walk arm in arm *¡Qué va!* / Nonsense! *¿Cómo le va?* / How goes it? How are you?

Cuando el gato va a sus devociones, bailan los ratones. / When the cat is away, the mice will play.

ser / to be

Present Participle: *siendo*   Past Participle: *sido*

THE SEVEN SIMPLE TENSES		THE SEVEN COMPOUND TENSES	
Singular	**Plural**	**Singular**	**Plural**
Present Indicative		Present Perfect Indicative	
soy	somos	he sido	hemos sido
eres	sois	has sido	habéis sido
es	son	ha sido	han sido
Imperfect Indicative		Pluperfect OR Past Perfect Indicative	
era	éramos	había sido	habíamos sido
eras	erais	habías sido	habíais sido
era	eran	había sido	habían sido
Preterit		Past Anterior OR Preterit Perfect	
fui	fuimos	hube sido	hubimos sido
fuiste	fuisteis	hubiste sido	hubisteis sido
fue	fueron	hubo sido	hubieron sido
Future		Future Perfect OR Future Anterior	
seré	seremos	habré sido	habremos sido
serás	seréis	habrás sido	habréis sido
será	serán	habrá sido	habrán sido
Conditional		Conditional Perfect	
sería	seríamos	habría sido	habríamos sido
serías	seríais	habrías sido	habríais sido
sería	serían	habría sido	habrían sido
Present Subjunctive		Present Perfect OR Past Subjunctive	
sea	seamos	haya sido	hayamos sido
seas	seáis	hayas sido	hayáis sido
sea	sean	haya sido	hayan sido
Imperfect Subjunctive		Pluperfect OR Past Perfect Subjunctive	
fuera	fuéramos	hubiera sido	hubiéramos sido
fueras	fuerais	hubieras sido	hubierais sido
fuera	fueran	hubiera sido	hubieran sido
OR		OR	
fuese	fuésemos	hubiese sido	hubiésemos sido
fueses	fueseis	hubieses sido	hubieseis sido
fuese	fuesen	hubiese sido	hubiesen sido

Imperative	
—	seamos
sé; no seas	sed; no seáis
sea	sean

Common Idiomatic Expressions Using this Verb

Dime con quien andas y te diré quien eres. / Tell me who your friends are and I will tell you who you are.
es decir / that is, that is to say; *Si yo fuera usted* . . . / If I were you . . .
¿Qué hora es? / What time is it? *Es la una.* / It is one o'clock. *Son las dos.* / It is two o'clock.

§7.8 INFINITIVES DEFINITION

In English, an infinitive is identified as a verb with the preposition "to" in front of it: to talk, to eat, to live. In Spanish, an infinitive is identified by its ending; those that end in *-ar, -er, -ir: hablar* (to talk, to speak), *comer* (to eat), *vivir* (to live).

Negation

To make an infinitive negative, place *no* in front of it.

No entrar. / Do not enter.

As a Verbal Noun

A verbal noun is a verb used as a noun. In Spanish, an infinitive may be used as a noun. This means that an infinitive may be used as a subject, a direct object, a predicate noun, or object of a preposition.

- As a subject:

  Ser o no ser es la cuestión. / To be or not to be is the question.
  El estudiar es bueno. OR *Estudiar es bueno.* / Studying (to study) is good.

  Here, when the infinitive is a subject and it begins the sentence, you may use the definite article *el* in front of the infinitive or you may omit it.
  If the sentence does not begin with the infinitive, do not use the definite article *el* in front of it:

  Es bueno estudiar. / It is good to study.

- As a direct object:

  No deseo comer. / I do not want to eat.

- As a predicate noun:

  Ver es creer. / Seeing is believing (To see is to believe).

- As object of a preposition:

  después de llegar. / after arriving.

  Here, the infinitive (verbal noun) *llegar* is object of the preposition de.

In Spanish, an infinitive is ordinarily used after such verbs as *dejar, hacer, mandar,* and *permitir* with no preposition needed:

Luis dejó caer sus libros. / Louis dropped his books.
Mi madre me hizo leerlo. / My mother made me read it.
Mi profesor me permitió hacerlo. / My teacher permitted me to do it.

Note that when *dejar* is followed by the preposition *de* it means to stop or to cease:

Luis dejó de trabajar. / Louis stopped working.

The verb *pensar* is directly followed by an infinitive with no preposition required in front of the infinitive when its meaning is "to intend:"

Pienso ir a Chile. / I intend to go to Chile.

Ordinarily, the infinitive form of a verb is used right after a preposition:

Antes de estudiar, Rita telefoneó a su amiga Beatriz. / Before studying, Rita telephoned her friend Beatrice.
El alumno salió de la sala de clase sin decir nada. / The pupil left the classroom without saying anything.

The infinitive form of a verb is ordinarily used after certain verbs of perception, such as *ver* and *oír:*

Las vi salir. / I saw them go out.
Las oí cantar. / I heard them singing.

After *al,* a verb is used in the infinitive form:

Al entrar en la escuela, Dorotea fue a su clase de español. / Upon entering the school, Dorothy went to her Spanish class.

The perfect infinitive (also known as the past infinitive) is formed by using *haber* in its infinitive form + the past participle of the main verb:

haber hablado / to have spoken
haber comido / to have eaten
haber escrito / to have written

§8.

Adverbs

DEFINITION

An adverb is a word that modifies a verb, an adjective, or another adverb.

§8.1 FORMATION

An adverb is regularly formed by adding the ending *mente* to the feminine singular form of an adjective.

lento, lenta / *lentamente:* slow / slowly
rápido, rápida / *rápidamente:* rapid / rapidly

If the form of the adjective is the same for the feminine singular and masculine singular *(fácil, feliz)*, add *mente* to that form.

> *fácil* (easy) / *fácilmente* (easily)
> *feliz* (happy) / *felizmente* (happily)

Note that an accent mark on an adjective remains when the adjective is changed to an adverb. And note that the Spanish ending *mente* is equivalent to the ending -ly in English.

An adverb remains invariable; that is to say, it does not agree in gender and number and therefore does not change in form.

There are many adverbs that do not end in *mente.* Some common ones are:

> | | |
> |---|---|
> | *abajo* / below | *arriba* / above |
> | *bien* / well | *mal* / badly |
> | *hoy* / today | *mañana* / tomorrow |
> | *siempre* / always | *nunca* / never |
> | *aquí* / here | *allí* / there |

The adverbial ending *ísimo*
Never use *muy* in front of *mucho.* Say *muchísimo:*

Elena trabaja muchísimo / Helen works a great deal; Helen works very, very much.

§8.2 COMPARISON

Regular comparison of adverbs
An adverb is compared regularly as an adjective.

María corre tan rápidamente como Elena / Mary runs as rapidly as Helen.
María corre menos rápidamente que Anita / Mary runs less rapidly than Anita.
María corre más rápidamente que Isabel / Mary runs more rapidly than Elizabeth.

Irregular comparative adverbs

mucho, poco / much, little: *Roberto trabaja mucho; Felipe trabaja poco.*
bien, mal / well, badly: *Juan trabaja bien; Lucas trabaja mal.*
más, menos / more, less: *Carlota trabaja más que Casandra; Elena trabaja menos que Marta.*
mejor, peor / better, worse: *Paula trabaja mejor que Anita; Isabel trabaja peor que Elena.*

§8.3 INTERROGATIVE ADVERBS COMMONLY USED

Some common interrogative adverbs are:

¿cómo? / how? *¿cuándo?* / when?
¿cuánto?, ¿cuánta?, ¿cuántos?, ¿cuántas? / how much? how many?
¿por qué? / why? *¿para qué?* / why? *¿dónde?* / where?
¿adónde? / where to? (to where?)

§8.4 NEGATIVE ADVERBS COMMONLY USED

jamás / ever, never, not ever
nada / nothing (*sin nada* / without anything); after *sin, nada* is used instead of *algo; Ella no quiere nada* / She does not want anything.

ni / neither, nor	*también* / also, too
ni . . . ni / neither . . . nor	*tampoco* / neither
ni siquiera / not even	*ni yo tampoco* / nor I either
nunca / never, not ever, ever	*unos cuantos, unas cuantas* /
siempre / always	a few, some, several

§8.5
SPECIAL
USES

Adverbs replaced by adjectives

An adverb may sometimes be replaced by an adjective whose agreement is with the subject, especially if the verb is one of motion:

Las muchachas van y vienen silenciosas. / **The girls come and go silently.**

Ahí, allí, allá

These three adverbs all mean "there" but they have special uses:

- *ahí* means there, not too far away from the person who says it:

  El libro que Ud. quiere está ahí sobre esa mesa. / **The book that you want is there on that table.**

- *allí* means there, farther away from the person who says it, or even at a remote distance:

  ¿Quiere Ud. ir a Chicago? Sí, porque mi padre trabaja allí. / **Do you want to go to Chicago? Yes, because my father works there.**

- *allá* means there, generally used with a verb of motion:

  Me gustaría mucho ir allá. / **I would like very much to go there.**
  Bueno, ¡vaya allá! / **Good, go there!**

Aquí and *acá*

These two adverbs both mean "here" but they have special uses:

- *aquí* means here, a place close to the person who says it:

  Aquí se habla español. / **Spanish is spoken here.**

- *acá* means here, a place close to the person who says it, but it is used with a verb of motion:

  Señor Gómez, ¡venga acá, por favor! / **Mr. Gómez, come here, please!**

Con, sin + noun

At times, an adverb can be formed by using the preposition *con* (with) or *sin* (without) + a noun:

con cuidado / carefully	*con dificultad* / with difficulty
sin cuidado / carelessly	*sin dificultad* / without difficulty

The adverb *recientemente* (recently) becomes *recién* before a past participle:

los recién llegados / **the ones recently arrived; the recently arrived (ones)**

Prepositions

A preposition is a word that connects words and, according to the thought expressed in the sentence, serves to indicate the relationship between the words.

a / at, to	*hacia* / toward
ante / before, in the presence of	*hasta* / until, up to, as far as
bajo / under	*menos* / except
con / with	*para* / for, in order to
contra / against	*por* / by, for
de / of, from	*salvo* / except, save
desde / after, from, since	*según* / according to
durante / during	*sin* / without
en / in, on	*sobre* / on, upon, over, above
entre / among, between	*tras* / after, behind

acerca de / about	*detrás de* / in back of, behind
además de / in addition to, besides	*en contra de* / against
alrededor de / around	*en cuanto a* / as far as
antes de / before	*en lugar de* / in place of, instead of
antes de nada / before anything	*en medio de* / in the middle of
antes de nadie / before anyone	*en vez de* / instead of
cerca de / near	*encima de* / on top of, upon
con rumbo a / in the direction of	*enfrente de* / opposite
debajo de / underneath	*frente a* / in front of
delante de / in front of	*fuera de* / outside of
dentro de / within, inside (of)	*junto a* / next to
después de / after	*lejos de* / far from
	por valor de / worth

Many prepositional phrases, such as the ones given above, would not be prepositional if the preposition *de* were not included in the phrase; without the preposition *de,* most of them are adverbs.

además / furthermore; *además de* / in addition to
alrededor / around; *alrededor de* / around
debajo / under; *debajo de* / underneath
lejos / far, far off; *lejos de* / far from

119

The use of the preposition *de* with these adverbs, and others, changes the part of speech to a preposition, as in such prepositional phrases as:

lejos de la escuela / far from the school
alrededor de la casa / around the house

Generally speaking, prepositions require a noun or a pronoun right after them (sometimes an infinitive, as in *sin decir nada* / without saying anything).

§9.4
USES OF PREPOSITIONS

Generally speaking, prepositions are used in the following categories:

> preposition + a noun: *con María* / with Mary;
>   *con mi amigo* / with my friend
> preposition + a pronoun: *para ella* / for her;
>   *para usted* / for you
> preposition + infinitive: *sin hablar* / without talking
> verb + preposition: *gozar de algo* / to enjoy something

§9.5
SPECIAL CASES

§9.5−1
Personal *a*

In Spanish, the preposition *a* is used in front of a noun direct object of a verb if the direct object is a person or something personified.

Conozco a su hermana Elena. / I know your sister Helen.
¿Conoce Ud. a Roberto? / Do you know Robert?
Llamo al médico. / I am calling the doctor.

The personal *a* is used in front of an indefinite pronoun when it is direct object of a verb and it refers to a person, for example: *nadie, ninguno (ninguna), alguien, alguno (alguna), quien*:

Mis padres están visitando a alguien en el hospital. / My parents are visiting someone in the hospital.
¿Ve Ud. a alguien? / Do you see anybody?
No veo a nadie. / I don't see anybody.

The personal *a* is used in front of a geographic name if it is used as direct object:

Este verano pensamos visitar a Colombia. / This summer we plan to visit Colombia.

But if the geographic place contains a definite article in front of it (which is part of its name), the personal *a* is not used:

¿Ha visitado Ud. la Argentina? / Have you visited Argentina?
La familia Gómez en Guadalajara quiere visitar los Estados Unidos. / The Gómez family in Guadalajara wants to visit the United States.

The personal *a* is used in front of a noun which is a domestic animal when personified and when it is direct object:

Quiero a mi gatito. / I love my kitten.

The personal *a* is not generally used with the verb *tener* when it means "to have:"

Tengo dos hermanas y dos hermanos. / I have two sisters and two brothers.

But when *tener* means "to hold," the personal *a* is generally used:

La enfermera tenía al niño en los brazos. / The nurse was holding the child in her arms.

§9.5–2
Para con

The prepositional expression *para con,* meaning "to" or "toward," in the sense of with respect to or as regards, is used to denote a mental attitude or feeling about a person:

Nuestra profesora de español es muy amable para con nosotros. / Our Spanish teacher is very kind to us.

§9.5–3
Para and *por*

These two prepositions are generally translated into English as "for."

Use *para* when you mean:

Destination:

Mañana salgo para Madrid. / Tomorrow I am leaving for Madrid.

Intended for:

Este vaso es para María y ese vaso es para José. / This glass is for Mary and that glass is for Joseph.
Esta taza es para café; es una taza para café. / This cup is for coffee; it is a coffee cup.

Purpose (in order to):

Estudio para llegar a ser médico. / I am studying in order to become a doctor.

A comparison of some sort:

Para ser norteamericano, habla español muy bien. / For an American, he speaks Spanish very well.

At some point in future time:

Esta lección es para mañana. / This lesson is for tomorrow.

Use *por* when you mean:

A length of time:

> *Me quedé en casa por tres días.* / I stayed at home for three days.

In exchange for:

> *¿Cuánto dinero me dará Ud. por mi trabajo?* / How much money will you give me for my work?

To send for:

> *Vamos a enviar por el médico.* / We are going to send for the doctor.

By:

> *Este libro fue escrito por dos autores.* / This book was written by two authors.
> *Quiero enviar esta carta por avión.* / I want to send this letter by air mail.

For the sake of, as an obligation, on someone's behalf:

> *Quiero hacerlo por usted.* / I want to do it for you.

Through:

> *Dimos un paseo por el parque.* / We took a walk through the park.

Along, by the edge of:

> *Anduvimos por la playa.* / We walked along the beach.

To fight for:

> *Luché por mi amigo.* / I fought for my friend.

Out of, because of + noun:

> *No quisieron hacerlo por miedo.* / They refused to do it out of (for) fear.

Per, when expressing frequency:

> *Los alumnos asisten a la escuela cinco días por semana.* / Students attend school five days a (per) week.

To go for someone or something:

> *Mi madre fue por Carmen.* / My mother went for (went to get) Carmen.
> *Mi madre fue por pan.* / My mother went for (went to get) bread.

To ask about, to inquire about, using *preguntar por:*

> *Pregunto por el médico.* / I am asking for the doctor.

§9.5–4
Por or *de*

The preposition *por* is sometimes translated into English as "by," although it has other meanings, such as "through," "for."

The preposition *de* is sometimes translated into English as "by" and it has other meanings, too, such as "of," "from," "in."

When using a passive meaning that expresses an action performed by someone or something, *por* is generally used.

Use the preposition *de* to express "by" when using a passive meaning if some emotion or feeling is expressed instead of an action.

> *La señora Gómez es respetada de todos los alumnos.* / Mrs. Gómez is respected by all the students.

§9.5–5
Special uses
of *para* and *por*

¿Para qué . . . ? and *¿Por qué . . . ?*

Both of these interrogatives mean "why" but they are not used interchangeably. If by "why" you mean for what reason, use *¿por qué . . . ?* If by "why" you mean for what purpose (what for?), use *¿para qué . . . ?*

> *Juanita, ¿por qué lloras?* / Jeanie, why (for what reason) are you crying?
> *Mamá, ¿para qué tenemos uñas?* / Mom, why (what for, for what purpose) do we have fingernails?

§10.

Conjunctions

DEFINITION

A conjunction is a word that connects words, phrases, clauses or sentences.

§10.1 COMMON CONJUNCTIONS

These terms are the most frequently used:

a fin de que / so that, in order that
a menos que / unless
antes (de) que / before
apenas . . . cuando / hardly, scarcely . . . when
así que / as soon as, after
aun / even, still
aunque / although
como / as, since, how
como si / as if
con tal (de) que / provided that
cuando / when
de manera que / so that
de modo que / so that, in such a way that
después (de) que / after
e / and
en cuanto / as soon as
hasta que / until
luego que / as soon as, after
mas / but
mas que / even if, however much
mientras / while
mientras que / while, so long as, as long as
ni / neither, nor (*ni . . . ni* / neither . . . nor)
ni siquiera / not even
a condición de que / on condition that
a pesar de que / in spite of
así . . . como / both . . . and
aun cuando / even if
caso que / in case that

como que / it seems that, apparently
como quiera que / although, since
con la condición de que / on condition that
dado caso que / supposing that
dado que / supposing that
de condición que / so as to
de suerte que / so that, in such a manner as
desde que / since
empero / yet, however, notwithstanding

These conjunctions may be less familiar to you:

y, pero, o, porque / and, but, or, because.
ni sólo . . . (sino) también / not only . . . but also
o / or (*o . . . o* / either . . . or)
o sea . . . o sea / either . . . or
para que / in order that, so that
pero / but
por cuanto / inasmuch as
porque / because
pues que / since
puesto que / although, since, inasmuch as, as long as
que / that, because
segun que / according as
si / if, whether
sin embargo / nevertheless, notwithstanding, however (in whatever way)

124

sin que / without
sino / but, but rather
sino que / but that, but rather that
siquiera / though, although, whether, or
tan pronto como / as soon as
u / or
y / and
ya . . . ya / now . . . now
ya que / since, seeing that
en caso de que / in case, in case that
en razón de que / for the reason that

entretanto que / meanwhile, while
más bien que / rather than
mientras tanto / meanwhile
no bien . . . cuando / no sooner . . . than
por más que / no matter how, however much
por razón de que / for the reason that
salvo que / unless
siempre que / whenever, provided that
tan luego como / therefore
tanto . . . como / as much . . . as

§10.2
OTHER
CONJUNCTIONS

§10.2-1
Pero and sino

These two words are conjunctions and they both mean "but." Note the uses:

> Me gustaría venir a tu casa esta noche pero no puedo. / I would like to come to your house tonight but I can't.

Use sino to mean "but rather," "but on the contrary:"

> Pedro no es pequeño sino alto. / Peter is not short but tall.
> Mi automóvil no es amarillo sino blanco. / My car is not yellow but white.

Note that when you use sino the first part of the sentence is negative. Also note that sino may be followed by an infinitive:

> Pablo no quiere alquilar el automóvil sino comprarlo. / Paul does not want to rent the car but to buy it.

If a clause follows sino, use sino que:

> Pablo no alquiló el automóvil sino que lo compró. / Paul did not rent the car but bought it.

And note finally that sino is used instead of pero when you make a clear contrast between a negative thought in the first part of the sentence and a positive thought in the second part. If no contrast is made or intended, use pero:

> María no conoce al niño pero le habla. / Mary does not know the child but talks to him.

§10.2–2
Pero and *mas*

These two words are conjunctions and they both mean "but." In plays and poems an author may sometimes use *mas* instead of *pero*. In conversation and informal writing, *pero* is used. Note that *mas* with no accent mark means "but" and *más* (with the accent mark) means "more."

§10.2–3
O and *U*

These two words, which are conjunctions, mean "or." Use *o* normally but when a word that is right after *o* begins with *o* or *ho*, use *u:*

> *muchachos u hombres* / boys or men; *septiembre u octubre* / September or October

§10.2–4
Y and *E*

These two words, which are conjunctions, mean "and." Use *y* normally but when a word that is right after *y* begins with *i* or *hi*, use *e:*

> *María es bonita e inteligente.* / Mary is pretty and intelligent.
> *Fernando e Isabel; padre e hijo* / father and son
> *madre e hija* / mother and daughter

However, if *y* is followed by a word that begins with *hie*, keep *y:*

> *flores y hierba* / flowers and grass

Special Topics

§11.

Exclamatory *¡Qué . . . !* and *¡Tal . . . !*

In English, when we exclaim What a class! What a student! What an idea! or Such an idea! we use the indefinite article a or an. In Spanish, however, we do not use the indefinite article.

¡Qué clase! ¡Qué alumno! ¡Qué alumna! ¡Qué idea! OR *¡Tal idea!*

If an adjective is used to describe the noun, we generally use *más* or *tan* in front of the adjective, in order to intensify the exclamation.

¡Qué chica tan bonita! / What a pretty girl!
¡Qué libro más interesante! / What an interesting book!

When we use *¡Qué!* + an adjective, the meaning in English is "How . . . !"

¡Qué difícil es! / How difficult it is!

§12.

Idioms

> *¿Cuánto tiempo hace que* + present tense . . . ?

¿Cuánto tiempo hace que Ud. estudia español? / How long
  have you been studying Spanish?
¿Cuánto tiempo hace que Ud. espera el autobús? / How long
  have you been waiting for the bus?

Use the present tense of the verb when the action of
studying, waiting, etc. is still going on at the present.

> *¿Cuánto tiempo hacía que* + imperfect tense

If the action of the verb began in the past and ended in
the past, use the imperfect tense.

*¿Cuánto tiempo hacía que Ud. hablaba cuando yo entré en la
sala de clase?* / How long had you been talking when I entered
  into the classroom?

> *¿Desde cuándo* + present tense . . . ?

This is another way of asking: How long (since when) +
the present perfect tense in English, as given above.

¿Desde cuándo estudia Ud. español? / How long have you been
                                         studying Spanish?

Present tense + *desde hace* + length of time

Estudio español desde hace tres años. / I have been studying
                                           Spanish for three
                                           years.

> *¿Desde cuándo* + imperfect tense . . . ?

*¿Desde cuándo hablaba Ud. cuando yo entré en la sala de
clase?* / How long had you been talking when I entered into the
  classroom?

Imperfect tense + *desde hacía* + length of time

*(Yo) hablaba desde hacía una hora cuando Ud. entró en la sala
de clase* / I had been talking for one hour when you entered
  into the classroom.

128

> ### *Hace* + length of time + *que* + present tense

Hace tres años que estudio español. / I have been studying Spanish for three years.

Hace veinte minutos que espero el autobús. / I have been waiting for the bus for twenty minutes.

¿Cuántos años hace que Ud. estudia español? / How many years have you been studying Spanish?

¿Cuántas horas hace que Ud. mira la televisión? / How many hours have you been watching television?

> ### *Hacía* + length of time + *que* + imperfect tense

Hacía una hora que yo hablaba cuando Ud. entró en la sala de clase. / I had been talking for one hour when you entered the classroom.

> ### *Hay* and *hay que* + infinitive

The word *hay* is not a verb. Its English equivalent is: There is . . . or There are . . . .

Hay muchos libros en la mesa. / There are many books on the table.

Hay una mosca en la sopa. / There is a fly in the soup.

Hay que + infinitive is an impersonal expression that denotes an obligation and it is commonly translated into English as: One must . . . or It is necessary to . . .

Hay que estudiar para aprender. / It is necessary to study in order to learn.

> ### *Medio* and *mitad*

Both these words mean "half" but note the uses:
Medio is an adjective and it agrees with the noun it modifies:

Necesito media docena de huevos. / I need half a dozen eggs.

Llegaremos en media hora. / We will arrive in a half hour (in half an hour).

Medio is also used as an adverb:

Los caballos corrieron rápidamente y ahora están medio muertos. / The horses ran fast and now they are half dead.

Mitad is a feminine noun:

El alumno estudió la mitad de la lección. / The pupil studied half
(of) the lesson.

§12.2 COMMON EXPRESSIONS

with *a*

a bordo / on board
a caballo / on horseback
a cada instante / at every moment, at every turn
a casa / home (Use with a verb of motion; use *a casa* if you
are going to the house; use *en casa* if you are in the house.
a eso de / about, around

Llegaremos a Madrid a eso de las tres de la tarde. / We will
arrive in Madrid at about 3 o'clock in the afternoon.

a fines de / about the end of, around the end of

Estaremos en Madrid a fines de la semana. / We will be in
Madrid around the end of the week.

a mano / by hand
a mediados de / around the middle of

Estaremos en Málaga a mediados de julio. / We will be in
Málaga around the middle of July.

a menudo / often, frequently
a mi parecer / in my opinion
a pesar de / in spite of
a pie / on foot
a principios de / around the beginning of

Estaremos en México a principios de la semana que viene. / We
will be in Mexico around the beginning of next week.

a saltos / by leaps and bounds
a tiempo / on time
a través de / across, through
a veces / at times, sometimes
estar a punto de / to be about to

Estoy a punto de salir. / I am about to leave.

frente a / in front of
junto a / beside, next to
poco a poco / little by little
ser aficionado a / to be a fan of
uno a uno / one by one

with *a la*

a la derecha / to (on, at) the right
a la española / in the Spanish style
a la francesa / in the French style
a la italiana / in the Italian style
a la izquierda / to (on, at) the left
a la larga / in the long run
a la madrugada / at an early hour, at daybreak
a la semana / a week, per week
a la vez / at the same time

with *al*

al + infinitive / on, upon + present participle

> *Al entrar en la cocina, comenzó a comer.* / Upon entering into the kitchen, he began to eat.

al aire libre / outdoors, in the open air
al amanecer / at daybreak, at dawn
al anochecer / at nightfall, at dusk
al cabo / finally, at last
al cabo de / at the end of
al contrario / on the contrary
al día / current, up to date
al día siguiente / on the following day, on the next day
al fin / at last, finally
al lado de / next to, beside
al menos / at least
al mes / a month, per month
al parecer / apparently
al principio / at first
echar al correo / to mail, to post a letter

with *con*

con frecuencia / frequently
con los brazos abiertos / with open arms
con motivo de / on the occasion of
con mucho gusto / gladly, willingly, with much pleasure
con permiso / excuse me, with your permission
con rumbo a / in the direction of
ser amable con / to be kind to

with *cuanto, cuanta, cuantos, cuantas*

cuanto antes / as soon as possible

> ¿*Cuánto cuesta?* / How much is it? How much does it cost?

cuanto más . . . tanto más . . . / the more . . . the
more . . .

> *Cuanto más estudio tanto más aprendo.* / The more I study the
> more I learn.
> ¿*Cuántos años tiene Ud.?* / How old are you?

unos cuantos libros / a few books; *unas cuantas flores* / a
few flowers

with *dar* and *darse*

dar a / to face

> *El comedor da al jardín.* / The dining room faces the garden.

dar con algo / to find something, to come upon something

> *Esta mañana di con dinero en la calle.* / This morning I found
> money in the street.

dar con alguien / to meet someone, to run into someone, to
come across someone, to find someone

> *Anoche, di con mi amiga Elena en el cine.* / Last night I met my
> friend Helen at
> the movies.

dar contra / to hit against
dar de beber a / to give something to drink to
dar de comer a / to feed, to give something to eat to

> *Me gusta dar de comer a los pájaros en el parque.* / I like to
> feed the
> birds in
> the
> park.

dar en / to hit against, to strike against
dar la bienvenida / to welcome
dar la hora / to strike the hour
dar la mano a alguien / to shake hands with someone
dar las gracias a alguien / to thank someone
dar los buenos días a alguien / to say good morning (hello)
to someone
dar por + past participle / to consider

> *Lo doy por perdido.* / I consider it lost.

dar recuerdos a / to give one's regards (best wishes) to
dar un abrazo / to embrace
dar un paseo / to take a walk
dar un paseo a caballo / to go horseback riding
dar un paseo en automóvil (en coche) / to go for a drive
dar un paseo en bicicleta / to ride a bicycle
dar una vuelta / to go for a short walk, to go for a stroll
dar unas palmadas / to clap one's hands
dar voces / to shout
darse cuenta de / to realize, to be aware of, to take into account
darse la mano / to shake hands with each other
darse prisa / to hurry

---

with *de*

acabar de + infinitive / to have just + past participle

   María acaba de llegar. / Mary has just arrived.
   María acababa de llegar. / Mary had just arrived.

acerca de / about, concerning
alrededor de / around
alrededor de la casa / around the house
antes de / before
aparte de / aside from
billete de ida y vuelta / round-trip ticket
cerca de / near, close to
de abajo / down, below
de acuerdo / in agreement, in accord
de aquí en adelante / from now on
de arriba / upstairs
de arriba abajo / from top to bottom
de ayer en ocho días / a week from yesterday
de balde / free, gratis
de broma / jokingly
de buena gana / willingly
de cuando en cuando / from time to time
de día / by day, in the daytime
de día en día / from day to day
de esa manera / in that way
de ese modo / in that way
de esta manera / in this way
de este modo / in this way
de hoy en adelante / from today on, from now on
de hoy en ocho días / a week from today

de la mañana / in the morning (Use this when a specific time is mentioned)

> *Tomo el desayuno a las ocho de la mañana.* / I have breakfast at 8 o'clock in the morning.

de la noche / in the evening (Use this when a specific time is mentioned.)

> *Mi amigo llega a las nueve de la noche.* / My friend is arriving at 9 o'clock in the evening.

de la tarde / in the afternoon (Use this when a specific time is mentioned)

> *Regreso a casa a las cuatro de la tarde.* / I am returning home at 4 o'clock in the afternoon.

de madrugada / at dawn, at daybreak
de mal humor / in bad humor, in a bad mood
de mala gana / unwillingly
de memoria / by heart (memorized)
de moda / in fashion
de nada / you're welcome
de ningún modo / no way, in no way, by no means
de ninguna manera / no way, in no way, by no means
de noche / by night, at night, during the night
de nuevo / again
de otra manera / in another way
de otro modo / otherwise
de pie / standing
de prisa / in a hurry
de pronto / suddenly
de repente / all of a sudden
de rodillas / kneeling, on one's knees
de todos modos / anyway, in any case, at any rate
de uno en uno / one by one
de veras / really, truly
de vez en cuando / from time to time
ir de compras / to go shopping
no hay de qué / you're welcome, don't mention it
un poco de / a little (of)
un poco de azúcar / a little sugar

---

with *decir*

---

decirle al oído / to whisper in one's ears
dicho y hecho / no sooner said than done

Es decir . . . / That is to say . . .
querer decir / to mean

> *¿Qué quiere decir este muchacho?* / What does this boy mean?

---

with *día, días*

al día / current, up to date
al romper el día / at daybreak
algún día / someday
de día en día / day by day
día por día / day by day
estar al día / to be up to date
hoy día / nowadays
por día / by the day, per day
quince días / two weeks
un día de éstos / one of these days

---

with *en*

en bicicleta / by bicycle
en broma / jokingly, in fun
en cambio / on the other hand
en casa / at home (Use *en casa* if you are in the house; use
   a casa with a verb of motion, if you are going to the house)

> *Me quedo en casa esta noche.* / I am staying home tonight.
> *Salgo de la escuela y voy a casa.* / I'm leaving school and I'm
>   going home.

en casa de / at the house of

> *María está en casa de Elena.* / Mary is at Helen's house.

en caso de / in case of
en coche / by car
en cuanto / as soon as
en cuanto a / as for, with regard to, in regard to
en efecto / as a matter of fact, in fact
en este momento / at this moment
en lo alto de / on top of it, at the top of, up
en lugar de / in place of, instead of
en medio de / in the middle of
en ninguna parte / nowhere
en punto / sharp, exactly (telling time)

> *Son las dos en punto.* / It is two o'clock sharp.

en seguida / immediately, at once
en todas partes / everywhere
en vano / in vain
en vez de / instead of
en voz alta / in a loud voice
en voz baja / in a low voice

---

with *estar*

está bien / all right, okay
estar a punto de + infinitive / to be about + infinitive

> *Estoy a punto de salir.* / I am about to go out.

estar conforme con / to be in agreement with
estar de acuerdo / to agree
estar de acuerdo con / to be in agreement with
estar de boga / to be in fashion, to be fashionable
estar de buenas / to be in a good mood
estar de pie / to be standing
estar de vuelta / to be back
estar para + infinitive / to be about to

> *Estoy para salir.* / I am about to go out.

estar por / to be in favor of
no estar para bromas / not to be in the mood for jokes

---

with *haber*

ha habido . . . / there has been . . . , there have been . . .
había . . . / there was . . . , there were . . .
habrá . . . / there will be . . .
habría . . . / there would be . . .
hubo . . . / there was . . . , there were . . .

---

with *hacer* and *hacerse*

hace poco / a little while ago
hace un año / a year ago
Hace un mes que partió el señor Molina. / Mr. Molina left one month ago.
hace una hora / an hour ago
hacer daño a alguien / to harm someone
hacer el baúl / to pack one's trunk
hacer el favor de + infinitive / please

> *Haga Ud. el favor de entrar.* / Please come in.

hacer el papel de / to play the role of
hacer falta / to be wanting, lacking, needed
hacer la maleta / to pack one's suitcase
hacer pedazos / to smash, to break, to tear into pieces
hacer un viaje / to take a trip
hacer una broma / to play a joke
hacer una pregunta / to ask a question
hacer una visita / to pay a visit
hacerle falta / to need

> *A Juan le hace falta un lápiz.* / John needs a pencil.

hacerse / to become

> *Elena se hizo dentista.* / Helen became a dentist.

hacerse daño / to hurt oneself, to harm oneself
hacerse tarde / to be getting late

> *Vámonos; se hace tarde.* / Let's leave; it's getting late.

with *hasta*

hasta ahora / until now
hasta aquí / until now, up to here
hasta después / see you later, until later
hasta entonces / see you then, see you later, up to that
time, until that time
hasta la vista / see you again
hasta luego / see you later, until later
hasta mañana / see you tomorrow, until tomorrow

with *lo*

a lo largo de / along
a lo lejos / in the distance
a lo menos / at least
lo bueno / what is good, the good part

> *¡Lo bueno que es!* / How good it is!
> *¡Lo bien que está escrito!* / How well it is written!

lo de + infinitive, adverb, or noun / "that matter of . . .",
"that business of . . ."
lo escrito / what is written
lo malo / what is bad, the bad part
lo más pronto posible / as soon as possible
lo mejor / what is best, the best part
lo primero que debo decir / the first thing I must say

lo simpático / whatever is kind
por lo contrario / on the contrary
por lo menos / at least
por lo pronto / in the meantime, for the time being
¡Ya lo creo! / I should certainly think so!

with *luego*

desde luego / naturally, of course, immediately
hasta luego / see you later, so long
luego luego / right away
luego que / as soon as, after

with *mañana*

ayer por la mañana / yesterday morning
de la mañana / in the morning (Use this when a specific time is mentioned):

> *Voy a tomar el tren a las seis de la mañana.* / I am going to take the train at six o'clock in the morning.

mañana por la mañana / tomorrow morning
mañana por la noche / tomorrow night
mañana por la tarde / tomorrow afternoon
pasado mañana / the day after tomorrow
por la mañana / in the morning (Use this when no exact time is mentioned):

> *El señor Pardo llega por la mañana.* / Mr. Pardo is arriving in the morning.

por la mañana temprano / early in the morning

with *mismo*

ahora mismo / right now
al mismo tiempo / at the same time
allá mismo / right there
aquí mismo / right here
así mismo / the same, the same thing
el mismo de siempre / the same old thing
eso mismo / that very thing
hoy mismo / this very day
lo mismo / the same, the same thing
lo mismo da / it makes no difference, it amounts to the same thing
lo mismo de siempre / the same old story
lo mismo que / the same as, as well as
por lo mismo / for the same reason

---

with *no*

Creo que no. / I don't think so, I think not.
No es verdad. / It isn't so, It isn't true; *¿No es verdad?* / Isn't that so?
No hay de qué. / You're welcome.
No hay remedio. / There's no way. It cannot be helped.
No importa. / It doesn't matter.
No + verb + *más que* + amount of money

> *No tengo más que un dólar.* / I have only one dollar.

todavía no / not yet
ya no / no longer

---

with *para*

estar para + infinitive / to be about to, to be at the point of

> *El autobús está para salir.* / The bus is about to leave.

para con / to, toward

> *Nuestra profesora de español es muy amable para con nosotros.* / Our Spanish teacher is very kind to us.

para eso / for that matter
para mí / for my part
para que / in order that, so that
para ser / in spite of being

> *Para ser tan viejo, él es muy ágil.* / In spite of being so old, he is very agile.

para siempre / forever
un vaso para agua / a water glass; *una taza para café* / a coffee cup

---

with *poco*

a poco / in a short while, presently
dentro de poco / in a short while, in a little while
en pocos días / in a few days
poco a poco / little by little
poco antes / shortly before
poco después / shortly after
por poco / nearly, almost
un poco de / a little (of)

> *Quisiera un poco de azúcar.* / I would like a little sugar.

---
with *por*
---

acabar por + infinitive / to end up by + present participle

> *Mi padre acabó por comprarlo.* / My father finally ended up by
> buying it.

al por mayor / wholesale
al por menor / retail (sales)
ayer por la mañana / yesterday morning
ayer por la noche / yesterday evening
ayer por la tarde / yesterday afternoon
estar por / to be in favor of
mañana por la mañana / tomorrow morning
mañana por la noche / tomorrow night, tomorrow evening
mañana por la tarde / tomorrow afternoon
por ahora / for just now, for the present
por aquí / this way, around here
por avión / by air mail
por consiguiente / consequently
por desgracia / unfortunately
por Dios / for God's sake
por ejemplo / for example
por el contrario OR *por lo contrario* / on the contrary
por escrito / in writing
por eso / for that reason, therefore
por favor / please

> *Entre, por favor.* / Come in, please.

por fin / at last, finally
por hora / by the hour, per hour
por la mañana / in the morning
por la noche / in the evening
por la noche temprano / early in the evening
por la tarde / in the afternoon
por lo común / commonly, generally, usually
por lo general / generally, usually
por lo menos / at least
por lo tanto / consequently, therefore
por lo visto / apparently
por mi parte / as for me, as far as I am concerned
por poco / nearly, almost
por semana / by the week, per week
por supuesto / of course
por teléfono / by phone
por todas partes / everywhere

with *pronto*

al pronto / at first
de pronto / suddenly
lo más pronto posible / as soon as possible
por de pronto / for the time being
por el pronto OR *por lo pronto* / in the meantime, for the
   time being
tan pronto como / as soon as

with *que*

Creo que no / I don't think so, I think not.
Creo que sí / I think so.
el año que viene / next year
la semana que viene / next week
¡Qué lástima¡ / What a pity!
¡Qué le vaya bien! / Good luck!
¡Qué lo pase Ud. bien! / Good luck! (I wish you a good
   outcome!)

with *ser*

Debe de ser . . . / It is probably . . .
Debe ser . . . / It ought to be . . .
Es de mi agrado / It's to my liking.
Es hora de . . . / It is time to . . .
Es lástima OR *Es una lástima* / It's a pity; It's too bad.
Es que . . . / The fact is . . .
para ser / in spite of being

   Para ser tan viejo, él es muy ágil. / In spite of being so old, he
                               is very nimble.

sea lo que sea / whatever it may be
ser aficionado a / to be a fan of

   Soy aficionado al béisbol. / I'm a baseball fan.

ser amable con / to be kind to

   Mi profesora de español es amable conmigo. / My Spanish
   teacher is kind to me.

ser todo oídos / to be all ears

   Te escucho; soy todo oídos. / I'm listening to you; I'm all ears.

with *sin*

sin aliento / out of breath
sin cuidado / carelessly
sin duda / without a doubt, undoubtedly
sin ejemplo / unparalleled, nothing like it
sin embargo / nevertheless, however
sin falta / without fail
sin novedad / nothing new, same as usual

with *tener*

¿Cuántos años tienes?

> *¿Cuántos años tiene Ud.?* / How old are you?
> *Tengo diez y seis años.* / I am sixteen years old.

¿Qué tienes?

> *¿Qué tiene Ud.?* / What's the matter? What's the matter with you?
> *No tengo nada.* / There's nothing wrong; There's nothing the matter (with me).

tener algo que hacer / to have something to do
tener calor / to feel (to be) warm (persons)
tener cuidado / to be careful
tener dolor de cabeza / to have a headache
tener dolor de estómago / to have a stomach ache
tener éxito / to be successful
tener frío / to feel (to be) cold (persons)
tener ganas de + infinitive / to feel like + present participle

> *Tengo ganas de tomar un helado.* / I feel like having an ice cream.

tener gusto en + infinitive / to be glad + infinitive

> *Tengo mucho gusto en conocerle.* / I am very glad to meet you.

tener hambre / to feel (to be) hungry
tener la bondad de / please; please be good enough to . . .

> *Tenga la bondad de cerrar la puerta.* / Please close the door.

tener la culpa de algo / to take the blame for something, to be to blame for something

> *Tengo la culpa de eso.* / I am to blame for that.

tener lugar / to take place

> *El accidente tuvo lugar anoche.* / The accident took place last night.

tener miedo de / to be afraid of
tener mucha sed / to feel (to be) very thirsty (persons)
tener mucho calor / to feel (to be) very warm (persons)
tener mucho frío / to feel (to be) very cold (persons)
tener mucho que hacer / to have a lot to do
tener poco que hacer / to have little to do
tener prisa / to be in a hurry
tener que + infinitive / to have + infinitive

   Tengo que estudiar. / I have to study.

tener razón / to be right

   Ud. tiene razón. / You are right.

no tener razón / to be wrong

   Ud. no tiene razón. / You are wrong.

tener sed / to feel (to be) thirsty (persons)
tener sueño / to feel (to be) sleepy
tener suerte / to be lucky

---

with *todo, toda, todos, todas*

a todo / at most
a todo correr / at full speed
ante todo / first of all, in the first place
así y todo / in spite of everything
de todos modos / anyway, in any case, at any rate
en un todo / in all its parts
en todo y por todo / in each and every way
ir a todo correr / to run by leaps and bounds
por todo / throughout
sobre todo / above all, especially
toda la familia / the whole family
todas las noches / every night
todas las semanas / every week
todo el mundo / everybody
todos cuantos / all those that
todos los años / every year
todos los días / every day

---

with *vez* and *veces*

a la vez / at the same time
a veces / sometimes, at times
alguna vez / sometime

algunas veces / sometimes
cada vez / each time
cada vez más / more and more (each time)
de vez en cuando / from time to time
dos veces / twice, two times
en vez de / instead of
muchas veces / many times
otra vez / again, another time, once more
raras veces / few times, rarely
tal vez / perhaps
una vez / once, one time
una vez más / once more, one more time
unas veces / sometimes
varias veces / several times

with *y*

dicho y hecho / no sooner said than done
sano y salvo / safe and sound
un billete de ida y vuelta / round-trip ticket
¿Y bien? / And then? And so? So what?
y eso que / even though
y por si eso fuera poco . . . / and as if that were not
   enough . . .

with *ya*

¡Hazlo ya! ¡Hágalo ya! / Do it now!
no ya . . . sino / not only . . . but also
¡Pues ya! / Of course! Certainly!
si ya . . . / if only . . .
¡Ya lo creo! / I should certainly think so! Of course!
Ya lo veré. / I'll see to it.
ya no / no longer
Ya pasó. / It's all over now.
ya que / since, as long as, seeing that . . .
¡Ya se ve! / Yes, indeed!
¡Ya voy! / I'm coming! I'll be there in a second!

§13.

Dates, Days, Months, Seasons

¿Cuál es la fecha? / What's the date?
¿Cuál es la fecha de hoy? / What's the date today?
Es el primero de junio. / It is June first.
Es el dos de mayo. / It is May second.

Note that when stating the date, in Spanish we use *el primero,* which is an ordinal number, for the first day of any month. To state all other dates, use the cardinal numbers: *Hoy es el dos de enero, el tres de febrero, el cuatro de marzo,* etc.

¿A cuántos estamos hoy? / What's the date today?
Estamos a cinco de abril. / It's April 5th.

When stating a date, the English word "on" is expressed in Spanish by using the definite article *el* in front of the date:

María nació el cuatro de julio. / Mary was born on the fourth of July.

- When stating the year, in Spanish we use thousand and hundreds:

el año mil novecientos ochenta y seis / the year 1986

This is very different from English, which is usually stated as nineteen eighty or nineteen hundred eighty. In Spanish we must state *mil* (one thousand) + *novecientos* (nine hundred): *mil novecientos setenta y nueve* (1979), *mil novecientos ochenta y uno* (1981).

- To sum up: *Hoy es sábado, el veintidós de agosto, mil novecientos ochenta y siete.* / Today is Saturday, August 22, 1987.

- The days of the week, which are all masculine, are:

> *domingo* / Sunday; *lunes* / Monday; *martes* / Tuesday; *miércoles* / Wednesday; *jueves* / Thursday; *viernes* / Friday; *sábado* / Saturday.

- In Spanish, the days of the week are ordinarily not capitalized. In newspapers, magazines, business letters, and elsewhere, you sometimes see them capitalized.

- When stating the day of the week in English we may use "on," but in Spanish we use *el* or *los* in front of the day of the week.

  > *el lunes* / on Monday; *los lunes* / on Mondays

  Note that the days of the week whose last letter is *s* do not change in the plural: *el martes / los martes; el miércoles / los miércoles.* BUT: *el sábado / los sábados; el domingo / los domingos.*

  > *¿Qué día es?* / What day is it?
  > *¿Qué día es hoy?* / What day is it today?
  > *Hoy es lunes.* / Today is Monday.

§13.3 MONTHS

- The months of the year, which are all masculine, are:

  > *enero* / January; *febrero* / February; *marzo* / March; *abril* / April; *mayo* / May; *junio* / June; *julio* / July; *agosto* / August; *septiembre* / September; *octubre* / October; *noviembre* / November; *diciembre* / December.

- In Spanish, the months of the year are ordinarily not capitalized. In newspapers, magazines, business letters, and elsewhere, you sometimes see them capitalized.
- To say in + the name of the month, use *en: en enero* / in January; OR: *en el mes de enero* / in the month of January
- The plural of *el mes* is *los meses.*

§13.4 SEASONS

- The seasons of the year *(las estaciones del año)* are:

  > *la primavera* / spring; *el verano* / summer; *el otoño* / autumn, fall; *el invierno* / winter.

- In Spanish, the seasons of the year are not capitalized.
- The definite article usually precedes a season of the year:

  > *¿En qué estación hace frío?* / In what season is it cold?
  > *Generalmente, hace frío en el invierno.* / Generally, it is cold in winter.

§14.

Telling Time

Son las tres de la tarde.
   OR:
Son las tres de la mañana.

¿Qué hora es? / **What time is it?**
Es la una. / **It is one o'clock.**

Note that the 3rd person singular of *ser* is used because the time is one (o'clock), which is singular.

Son las dos. / **It is two o'clock.**

Note that the 3rd person plural of *ser* is used because the time is two (o'clock), which is more than one.

Son las tres, son las cuatro. / **It is three o'clock, it is four o'clock.**

When the time is a certain number of minutes after the hour, the hour is stated first *(Es la una)* + *y* + the number of minutes:

Es la una y cinco. / **It is five minutes after one o'clock (It is 1:05).**
Son las dos y diez. / **It is ten minutes after two o'clock (It is 2:10).**

When the hour is a quarter after, you can express it by using either *y cuarto* or *y quince (minutos)*:

Son las dos y cuarto **OR** *Son las dos y quince (minutos).* / **It is 2:15.**

When it is half past the hour, you can express it by using either *y media* or *y treinta (minutos)*:

Son las dos y media **OR** *Son las dos y treinta.* / **It is 2:30.**

When the time is a certain number of minutes of (to, toward, before) the hour, state the hour that it will be + *menos* + the number of minutes. If it is 15 minutes before the hour, use *menos cuarto* (a quarter of).

Son las cinco menos veinte. / **It is twenty minutes to five OR It is 4:40.**
Son las cuatro menos cuarto. / **It is a quarter of (to) four OR It is 3:45.**

When you are not telling what time it is and you want only to say at a certain time, merely say:

a la una, a las dos, a las tres / **at one o'clock, at two o'clock, at three o'clock**

a la una y cuarto / at 1:15; *a las cuatro y media* / at 4:30
¿A qué hora va Ud. a la clase de español? / At what time do
you go to Spanish class?
Voy a la clase a las dos y veinte. / I go to class at 2:20.
¿A qué hora toma Ud. el almuerzo? / At what time do you have
lunch?
Tomo el almuerzo a las doce en punto. / I have lunch at exactly
twelve o'clock.
¿A qué hora toma Ud. el autobús para ir a la escuela? / At what
time do you take the bus to go to school?
Tomo el autobús a las ocho en punto. / I take the bus at eight
o'clock sharp.
¿Llega Ud. a la escuela a tiempo? / Do you arrive at school on
time?
Llego a la escuela a eso de las ocho y media. / I arrive at school
at about 8:30.

When you state what time it is or at what time you are
going to do something, sometimes you have to make it
clear whether it is in the morning (A.M.), in the afternoon
(P.M.), or in the evening (P.M.):

Tomo el tren a las ocho de la noche. / I am taking the train at
8:00 P.M. (at eight o'clock in the evening).
Tomo el tren a las ocho de la mañana. / I am taking the train at
8:00 A.M. (at eight o'clock in the morning).
Tomo el tren a las cuatro de la tarde. / I am taking the train at
4:00 P.M. (at four o'clock in the afternoon).
Tomo el tren a las tres de la madrugada. / I am taking the train
at 3:00 A.M. (at three o'clock in the morning).

Note that in Spanish we say *de la madrugada* (before
daylight hours) instead of *de la noche* if the time is between
midnight and the break of dawn.

¿Qué hora es? / What time is it? *Es mediodía.* / It is noon.
¿Qué hora es? / What time is it? *Es medianoche.* / It is midnight.
¿A qué hora toma Ud. el almuerzo? / At what time do you have
lunch? *Tomo el almuerzo a mediodía* (OR *al mediodía*).
¿A qué hora se acuesta Ud. por lo general? / At what time do
you generally get to bed? *Generalmente, me acuesto a
medianoche* (or *a la medianoche*).

When telling time in the past, use the imperfect indicative
tense of the verb *ser:*

Eran las dos cuando tomé el almuerzo hoy. / It was two o'clock
when I had lunch today.
Era la una cuando los vi. / It was one o'clock when I saw them.
¿Qué hora era cuando sus padres llegaron a casa? / What time
was it when your parents arrived home?
Eran las dos de la madrugada. / It was two in the morning.

The future tense is used when telling time in the future or when you wonder what time it is at present or when you want to state what time it probably is:

En algunos minutos serán las tres / In a few minutes it will be three o'clock.
¿Qué hora será? / I wonder what time it is.
Serán las seis. / It is probably six o'clock.

When wondering what time it was in the past or when stating what time it probably was in the past, use the conditional:

¿Qué hora sería? / I wonder what time it was? *Serían las seis cuando llegaron.* / It was probably six o'clock when they arrived.

When no specific time is stated and you merely want to say in the morning, in the afternoon, or in the evening, use the preposition *por* instead of *de:*

Los sábados estudio mis lecciones por la mañana, juego por la tarde, y salgo por la noche. / On Saturdays I study my lessons in the morning, I play in the afternoon, and I go out in the evening.

To express a little after the hour, state the hour + *y pico:*

Cuando salí eran las seis y pico. / When I went out it was a little after six o'clock.

To say about or around a particular time, say *a eso de* + the hour:

Te veré a eso de la una. / I will see you about one o'clock.
Te veré a eso de las tres. / I will see you around three o'clock.

Instead of using *menos* (of, to, toward, before the hour), you may use the verb *faltar,* which means to be lacking: *Faltan cinco minutos para las tres* / It's five minutes to three (in other words, five minutes are lacking before it is three o'clock). In this construction, which is idiomatic, note the use of the preposition *para.*

§14.2 "OFFICIAL" TIME EX- PRESSIONS

Finally, note another way to tell time, which is used on radio and TV, in railroad and bus stations, at airports, and at other places where many people gather. It is the 24-hour system around the clock.

When using the 24 hours around the clock, the stated time is perfectly clear and there is no need to say *de la madrugada, de la mañana, de la tarde,* or *de la noche.*

When using the 24-hour system around the clock, there is no need to use *cuarto, media, menos* or *y* (except when *y* is required in the cardinal number: *diez y seis*).

When you hear or see the stated time using this system, subtract 12 from the number that you hear or see. If the number is less than 12, it is A.M. time. Midnight is *veinticuatro horas.* This system uses the cardinal numbers.

---

trece horas / 1 P.M.
catorce horas / 2 P.M.
veinte horas / 8 P.M.
quince horas treinta / 15.30; 3:30 P.M.
veinte horas cuarenta y dos / 20.42; 8:42 P.M.
nueve horas diez / 09.10; 9:10 A.M.

---

§15.

Weather Expressions

with *hacer*

¿Qué tiempo hace? / What is the weather like?
Hace buen tiempo. / The weather is good.
Hace calor. / It is warm (hot).
Hace fresco hoy. / It is cool today.
Hace frío. / It is cold.
Hace mal tiempo. / The weather is bad.
Hace sol. / It is sunny.
Hace viento. / It is windy.
¿Qué tiempo hacía cuando Ud. salió esta mañana? / What
  was the weather like when you went out this morning?
Hacía mucho frío ayer por la noche. / It was very cold
  yesterday evening.
Hacía mucho viento. / It was very windy.
¿Qué tiempo hará mañana? / What will the weather be like
  tomorrow?
Se dice que hará mucho calor. / They say it will be very hot.

with *haber*

Hay lodo. / It is muddy. *Había lodo.* / It was muddy.
Hay luna. / The moon is shining. OR There is moonlight.
Había luna ayer por la noche. / There was moonlight
  yesterday evening.
¿Hay mucha nieve aquí en el invierno? / Is there much snow
  here in winter?
Hay neblina. / It is foggy; *Había mucha neblina.* / It was
  very foggy.
Hay polvo. / It is dusty. *Había mucho polvo.* / It was very
  dusty.

Other weather expressions

Está lloviendo ahora. / It is raining now.
Está nevando. / It is snowing.
Esta mañana llovía cuando tomé el autobús. / This morning
  it was raining when I took the bus.
Estaba lloviendo cuando tomé el autobús. / It was raining
  when I took the bus.

Estaba nevando cuando me desperté. / It was snowing
 when I woke up.
¿Nieva mucho aquí en el invierno? / Does it snow much
 here in winter?
Las estrellas brillan. / The stars are shining.
¿Le gusta a usted la lluvia? / Do you like rain?
¿Le gusta a usted la nieve? / Do you like snow?

§16.

Numbers

§16.1
CARDINAL
NUMBERS:
ZERO TO
ONE
HUNDRED
MILLION

0 *cero*
1 *uno, una*
2 *dos*
3 *tres*
4 *cuatro*
5 *cinco*
6 *seis*
7 *siete*
8 *ocho*
9 *nueve*
10 *diez*
11 *once*
12 *doce*
13 *trece*
14 *catorce*
15 *quince*
16 *dieciséis*
17 *diecisiete*
18 *dieciocho*
19 *diecinueve*
20 *veinte*
21 *veintiuno*
22 *veintidós*
23 *veintitrés*
24 *veinticuatro*
25 *veinticinco*
26 *veintiséis*
27 *veintisiete*
28 *veintiocho*
29 *veintinueve*
30 *treinta*
31 *treinta y uno, treinta y una*
32 *treinta y dos*, etc.

40 *cuarenta*
41 *cuarenta y uno, cuarenta y una*
42 *cuarenta y dos*, etc.

50 *cincuenta*
51 *cincuenta y uno, cincuenta y una*
52 *cincuenta y dos*, etc.

60 *sesenta*
61 *sesenta y uno, sesenta y una*
62 *sesenta y dos, etc.*

70 *setenta*
71 *setenta y uno, setenta y una*
72 *setenta y dos, etc.*

80 *ochenta*
81 *ochenta y uno, ochenta y una*
82 *ochenta y dos, etc.*

90 *noventa*
91 *noventa y uno, noventa y una*
92 *noventa y dos*, etc.

100 *ciento (cien)*
101 *ciento uno, ciento una*
102 *ciento dos*, etc.

200 *doscientos, doscientas*
300 *trescientos, trescientas*
400 *cuatrocientos, cuatrocientas*
500 *quinientos, quinientas*

153

600 *seiscientos, seiscientas*	2,000,000 *dos millones (de + noun)*
700 *setecientos, setecientas*	3,000,000 *tres millones (de + noun)*
800 *ochocientos, ochocientas*	100,000,000 *cien millones (de + noun)*
900 *novecientos, novecientas*	**Approximate numbers**
1,000 *mil*	*unos veinte libros* / about (some) twenty books
2,000 *dos mil*	
3,000 *tres mil, etc.*	
100,000 *cien mil*	*unas treinta personas* / about (some) thirty persons
200,000 *doscientos mil, doscientas mil*	
300,000 *trescientos mil, trescientas mil, etc.*	
1,000,000 *un millón (de + noun)*	

Simple arithmetical expressions	
dos y dos son cuatro	$2 + 2 = 4$
diez menos cinco son cinco	$10 - 5 = 5$
tres por cinco son quince	$3 \times 5 = 15$
diez dividido por dos son cinco	$10 \div 2 = 5$

§16.2 ORDINAL NUMBERS: FIRST TO TENTH

primero, primer, primera	first	1st
segundo, segunda	second	2nd
tercero, tercer, tercera	third	3rd
cuarto, cuarta	fourth	4th
quinto, quinta	fifth	5th
sexto, sexta	sixth	6th
séptimo, séptima	seventh	7th
octavo, octava	eighth	8th
noveno, novena	ninth	9th
décimo, décima	tenth	10th

Note that beyond 10th the cardinal numbers are used instead of the ordinal numbers, but when there is a noun involved, the cardinal number is placed after the noun:

el día 15, el día quince / the fifteenth day

Note also that in titles of monarchs, etc., the definite article is not used between the person's name and the number, as it is in English:

Alfonso XIII, Alfonso Trece / Alfonso the Thirteenth

And note that *noveno* changes to *nono* in such titles:

Luis IX, Luis Nono / Louis the Ninth

§17.

Synonyms

There are many Spanish words that are approximate in meaning to another. A list of these synonyms follows, along with the English counterparts.

acercarse (a), aproximarse (a) / to approach, to come near
acordarse (de), recordar / to remember
alabar, elogiar / to praise, to glorify, to eulogize
alimento, comida / food, nourishment
alumno (alumna), estudiante / pupil, student
andar, caminar / to walk
anillo, sortija / ring (finger)
antiguo (antigua), viejo (vieja) / ancient, old
asustar, espantar / to frighten, to terrify, to scare
atreverse (a), osar / to dare, to venture
aún, todavía / still, yet, even
ayuda, socorro, auxilio / aid, succor, help, assistance
barco, buque, vapor / boat, ship
bastante, suficiente / enough, sufficient
batalla, combate, lucha / battle, combat, struggle, fight
bonito (bonita), lindo (linda) / pretty
breve, corto (corta) / brief, short
burlarse de, mofarse de / to make fun of, to mock
camarero, mozo / waiter
campesino, rústico, labrador / farmer, peasant
cara, rostro, semblante / face
cariño, amor / affection, love
cocinar, cocer, guisar / to cook
comenzar, empezar, principiar / to begin, to start, to
   commence
comprender, entender / to understand, to comprehend
conquistar, vencer / to conquer, to vanquish
contento (contenta), feliz, alegre / content, happy, glad
contestar, responder / to answer, to reply
continuar, seguir / to continue
cruzar, atravesar / to cross
cuarto, habitación / room
cura, sacerdote / priest
chiste, chanza, broma / jest, joke, fun
dar un paseo, pasearse / to take a walk, to go for a walk
dar voces, gritar / to shout, to cry out
delgado, esbelto, flaco / thin, slender, slim, svelte
desafortunado, desgraciado / unfortunate
desaparecer, desvanecerse / to disappear, to vanish

desear, querer / to desire, to want, to wish
desprecio, desdén / scorn, disdain, contempt
diablo, demonio / devil, demon
diferente, distinto (distinta) / different, distinct
diversión, pasatiempo / diversion, pastime
echar, lanzar, tirar, arrojar / to throw, to lance, to hurl
elevar, levantar, alzar / to elevate, to raise, to lift
empleado (empleada), dependiente / employee, clerk
enojarse, enfadarse / to become angry, to become annoyed
enviar, mandar / to send
error, falta / error, mistake, fault
escoger, elegir / to choose, to select, to elect
esperar, aguardar / to wait for
esposa, mujer / wife, spouse
estrecho (estrecha), angosto (angosta) / narrow
famoso (famosa), célebre, ilustre / famous, celebrated,
    renowned, illustrious
fiebre, calentura / fever
grave, serio (seria) / serious, grave
habilidad, destreza / ability, skill, dexterity
hablador (habladora), locuaz / talkative, loquacious
halagar, lisonjear, adular / to flatter
hallar, encontrar / to find
hermoso (hermosa), bello (bella) / beautiful, handsome
igual, semejante / equal, alike, similar
invitar, convidar / to invite
irse, marcharse / to leave, to go away
joya, alhaja / jewel, gem
lanzar, tirar, echar / to throw, to lance, to hurl
lengua, idioma / language, idiom
lentamente, despacio / slowly
luchar, combatir, pelear, pugnar / to fight, to battle, to
    combat, to struggle
lugar, sitio / place, site
llevar, conducir / to take, to lead
maestro (maestra), profesor (profesora) / teacher, professor
marido, esposo / husband, spouse
miedo, temor / fear, dread
morir, fallecer, fenecer / to die, to expire
mostrar, enseñar / to show
nobleza, hidalguez, hidalguía / nobility
nunca, jamás / never
obtener, conseguir / to obtain, to get
odiar, aborrecer / to hate, to abhor
onda, ola / wave
país, nación / country, nation
pájaro, ave / bird

pararse, detenerse / to stop (oneself)
parecido, semejante / like, similar
pasar un buen rato, divertirse / to have a good time
pena, dolor / pain, grief
perezoso (perezosa), flojo (floja) / lazy
periódico, diario / newspaper
permiso, licencia / permission, leave
permitir, dejar / to permit, to allow, to let
poner, colocar / to put, to place
posponer, diferir, aplazar / to postpone, to defer, to put off, to delay
premio, galardón / prize, reward
quedarse, permanecer / to remain, to stay
rapidez, prisa, velocidad / rapidly, haste, speed, velocity
regresar, volver / to return (to a place)
rezar, orar / to pray
rogar, suplicar / to beg, to implore, to entreat
romper, quebrar / to break
sin embargo, no obstante / nevertheless, however
solamente, sólo / only
sorprender, asombrar / to surprise, to astonish
suceso, acontecimiento / happening, event
sufrir, padecer / to suffer, to endure
susto, espanto / fright, scare, dread
tal vez, acaso, quizá, quizás / maybe, perhaps
terminar, acabar, concluir / to terminate, to finish, to end
tonto (tonta), necio (necia) / foolish, stupid, idiotic
trabajo, tarea, obra / work, task
tratar de, intentar / to try to, to attempt
ya que, puesto que / since, inasmuch as

§18.

Antonyms

Here is a list of antonyms in Spanish, with the English translation of each word.

aburrirse / to be bored; *divertirse* / to have a good time
aceptar / to accept; *ofrecer* / to offer
acordarse de / to remember; *olvidar, olvidarse de* / to forget
admitir / to admit; / to deny
agradecido, agradecida / thankful; *ingrato, ingrata* /
   thankless
alejarse de / to go away from; *acercarse a* / to approach
algo / something; *nada* / nothing
alguien / someone; *nadie* / no one
alguno (algún) / some; *ninguno (ningún)* / none
amar / to love; *odiar* / to hate
amigo, amiga / friend; *enemigo, enemiga* / enemy
ancho, ancha / wide; *estrecho, estrecha* / narrow
antes (de) / before; *después (de)* / after
antiguo, antigua / ancient, old; *moderno, moderna* / modern
antipático, antipática / unpleasant; *simpático,*
   simpática / nice (people)
aparecer / to appear; *desaparecer* / to disappear
aplicado, aplicada / industrious; *flojo, floja* / lazy
apresurarse a / to hasten, to hurry; *tardar en* / to delay
aprisa / quickly; *despacio* / slowly
aquí / here; *allí* / there
arriba / above, upstairs; *abajo* / below, downstairs
ausente / absent; *presente* / present
bajar / to go down; *subir* / to go up
bajo, baja / low, short; *alto, alta* / high, tall
bien / well; *mal* / badly, poorly
bueno (buen), buena / good; *malo (mal)* / bad
caballero / gentleman; *dama* / lady
caliente / hot; *frío* / cold
caro, cara / expensive; *barato, barata* / cheap
cerca (de) / near; *lejos (de)* / far
cerrar / to close; *abrir* / to open
claro, clara / light; *oscuro, oscura* / dark
cobarde / cowardly; *valiente* / valiant, brave
cómico, cómica / comic, funny; *trágico, trágica* / tragic
comprar / to buy; *vender* / to sell
común / common; *raro, rara* / rare
con / with; *sin* / without
contra / against; *con* / with

corto, corta / short; *largo, larga* / long

costoso, costosa / costly, expensive; *barato, barata* / **cheap, inexpensive**

culpable / guilty, culpable; *inocente* / innocent

dar / to give; *recibir* / to receive

débil / weak, debilitated; *fuerte* / strong

dejar caer / to drop; *recoger* / to pick up

delante de / in front of; *detrás de* / in back of

delgado, delgada / thin; *gordo, gorda* / stout, fat

dentro / inside; *fuera* / outside

derrota / defeat; *victoria* / victory

descansar / to rest; *cansar* / to tire; *cansarse* / **to get tired**

descubrir / to uncover; *cubrir* / to cover

descuido / carelessness; *esmero* / meticulousness

desgraciado, desgraciada / unfortunate; *afortunado, afortunada* / fortunate

despertarse / to wake up; *dormirse* / to fall asleep

destruir / to destroy; *crear* / to create

desvanecerse / to disappear; *aparecer* / **to appear**

distinto, distinta / different; *semejante* / similar

dulce / sweet; *amargo* / bitter

duro, dura / hard; *suave, blando, blanda* / soft

elogiar / to praise; *censurar* / to criticize

empezar / to begin, to start; *terminar, acabar* / to end

encender / to light; *apagar* / to extinguish

encima (de) / on top; *debajo (de)* / under

entrada / entrance; *salida* / exit

esta noche / tonight, this evening; *anoche* / last night, yesterday evening

este / east; *oeste* / west

estúpido, estúpida / stupid; *inteligente* / intelligent

éxito / success; *fracaso* / failure

fácil / easy; *difícil* / difficult

fatigado, fatigada / tired; *descansado, descansada* / **rested**

feliz / happy; *triste* / sad

feo, fea / ugly; *hermoso, hermosa* / beautiful; *bello, bella* / beautiful

fin / end; *principio* / beginning

flaco, flaca / thin; *gordo, gorda* / fat

gastar / to spend (money); *ahorrar* / to save (money)

gigante / giant; *enano* / dwarf

grande (gran) / large, big; *pequeño, pequeña* / **small, little**

guerra / war; *paz* / peace

hablador, habladora / talkative; *taciturno, taciturna* / **silent, taciturn**

hablar / to talk, to speak; *callarse* / to keep silent

hembra / female; *macho* / male

ida / departure; *vuelta* / return (*ida y vuelta* / round trip)
ignorar / not to know; *saber* / to know
interesante / interesting; *aburrido, aburrida* / boring
inútil / useless; *útil* / useful
ir / to go; *venir* / to come
joven / young; *viejo, vieja* / old
jugar / to play; *trabajar* / to work
juventud / youth; *vejez* / old age
lejano / distant; *cercano* / nearby
lentitud / slowness; *rapidez* / speed
levantarse / to get up; *sentarse* / to sit down
libertad / liberty; *esclavitud* / slavery
limpio, limpia / clean; *sucio, sucia* / dirty
luz / light; *sombra* / shadow
llegada / arrival; *partida* / departure
llenar / to fill; *vaciar* / to empty
lleno, llena / full; *vacío, vacía* / empty
llorar / to cry, to weep; *reír* / to laugh
maldecir / to curse; *bendecir* / to bless
mañana / tomorrow; *ayer* / yesterday
más / more; *menos* / less
mejor / better; *peor* / worse
menor / younger; *mayor* / older
mentir / to lie; *decir la verdad* / to tell the truth
mentira / lie, falsehood; *verdad* / truth
meter / to put in; *sacar* / to take out
mismo, misma / same; *diferente* / different
mucho, mucha / much; *poco, poca* / little
nacer / to be born; *morir* / to die
natural / natural; *innatural* / unnatural
necesario / necessary; *innecesario* / unnecessary
negar / to deny; *otorgar* / to grant
noche / night; *día* / day
obeso, obesa / obese, fat; *delgado, delgada* / thin
obscuro, obscura / dark; *claro, clara* / light
odio / hate, hatred; *amor* / love
orgulloso / proud; *humilde* / humble
oriental / eastern; *occidental* / western
peligro / danger; *seguridad* / safety
perder / to lose; *ganar* / to win; *hallar* / to find
perezoso, perezosa / lazy; *diligente* / diligent
permitir / to permit; *prohibir* / to prohibit
pesado, pesada / heavy; *ligero, ligera* / light
ponerse / to put on (clothing); *quitarse* / to take off (clothing)
porvenir / future; *pasado* / past
posible / possible; *imposible* / impossible
pregunta / question; *respuesta, contestación* / answer

preguntar / to ask; *contestar* / to answer
presente / present; *ausente* / absent
prestar / to lend; *pedir prestado* / to borrow
primero (primer), primera / first; *último, última* / last
puesta del sol / sunset; *salida del sol* / sunrise
quedarse / to remain; *irse* / to leave, to go away
quizá(s) / maybe, perhaps; *seguro, cierto* / sure, certain
recto / straight; *tortuoso* / winding
rico, rica / rich; *pobre* / poor
riqueza / wealth; *pobreza* / poverty
rubio, rubia / blond; *moreno, morena* / brunette
ruido / noise; *silencio* / silence
sabio, sabia / wise; *tonto, tonta* / foolish
salir (de) / to leave (from); *entrar (en)* / to enter (in, into)
seco / dry; *mojado* / wet
separar / to separate; *juntar* / to join
sí / yes; *no* / no
siempre / always; *nunca* / never
subir / to go up; *bajar* / to go down
sucio / dirty; *limpio* / clean
sur / south; *norte* / north
temprano / early; *tarde* / late
tomar / to take; *dar* / to give
tonto / foolish; *listo* / clever
tranquilo / tranquil, peaceful; *turbulento* / restless, turbulent
unir / to unite; *desunir* / to disunite
usual / usual; *extraño, raro* / unusual
vida / life; *muerte* / death
virtud / virtue; *vicio* / vice
y / and, plus; *menos* / minus, less

§19.

Cognates

Another good way to increase your vocabulary is to become aware of cognates. A cognate is a word whose origin is the same as another word in other languages. There are many cognates in Spanish and English. Their spelling is sometimes identical or very similar in both languages. Most of the time, the meaning is the same or similar; sometimes they appear to be related because of the similar or identical spelling but they are not true cognates. Those are described as "false cognates"—for example, the Spanish word *actual* means present-day, not actual; the English word actual is expressed in Spanish as *real, verdadero, efectivo,* or *existente.* Also, the Spanish word *pan* means bread, not pan. The English word pan is *cacerola, cazuela,* or *sartén* in Spanish.

Generally speaking, Spanish words that have certain endings have equivalent endings in English.

SPANISH ENDING OF A WORD	EQUIVALENT ENGLISH ENDING OF A WORD
-ario	-ary
-ción	-tion
-dad	-ty
-fía	-phy
-ia	-y
-ía	-y
-io	-y
-ista	-ist
-mente	-ly
-orio	-ory
-oso	-ous

There are others, but the above seem to be the most common. Also note that Spanish words that begin with *es* are generally equivalent to an English word that begins with s. Just drop the *e* in the beginning of the Spanish word and you have a close equivalent to the spelling of an English word.

especial / special; *estudiante* / student

Here are examples to illustrate true cognates whose spellings are identical or similar:

actor / actor	*historia* / history
admiración / admiration	*hotel* / hotel
atención / attention	*idea* / idea
autoridad / authority	*invitación* / invitation
central / central	*manual* / manual
civilización / civilization	*nación* / nation
color / color	*naturalmente* / naturally
correctamente / correctly	*necesario* / necessary
chocolate / chocolate	*necesidad* / necessity
dentista / dentist	*novelista* / novelist
doctor / doctor	*piano* / piano
dormitorio / dormitory, bedroom	*posibilidad* / possibility
	radio / radio
escena / scene	*realidad* / reality
estúpido / stupid	*remedio* / remedy
famoso / famous	*sección* / section
farmacia / pharmacy	*sociedad* / society
finalmente / finally	*universidad* / university
fotografía / photography	*violín* / violin
generoso / generous	*vocabulario* / vocabulary
geografía / geography	

Tricky Words

actual / present, of the present time, of the present day

el anciano, la anciana / old (man or woman)

antiguo, antigua / former, old, ancient

la apología / eulogy, defense

la arena / sand

asistir a / to attend, to be present at

atender / to attend to, to take care of

el auditorio / audience

el bachiller, la bachillera /graduate of a secondary school; also means babbler

el bagaje / beast of burden, military equipment

la bala / bullet, shot, bale, ball

bizarro, bizarra / brave, gallant, generous

el campo / field, country(side), military camp

el carbón / coal, charcoal, carbon

el cargo / duty, post, responsibility, burden, load

la carta / letter (to mail)

el collar / necklace

colorado, colorada / red, ruddy

la complexión / temperament, constitution

la conferencia / lecture

la confianza / confidence, trust

la confidencia / secret, trust

constipado, constipada / head cold or common cold

la consulta / conference

convenir / to agree, to fit, to suit, to be suitable

la chanza / joke, fun

de / from, of

dé / give

la decepción / disappointment

el delito / crime

la desgracia / misfortune

el desmayo / fainting

diario, diaria / daily

el diario / diary, journal, daily newspaper

disfrutar / to enjoy

divisar / to perceive indistinctly

el dormitorio / bedroom, dormitory

el editor / publisher

embarazada / pregnant

emocionante / touching (causing an emotion)

esperar / to hope, to expect, to wait for

el éxito / success, outcome

la fábrica / factory
hay / there is, there are (idiomatic)
el idioma / language
ignorar / not to know, to be unaware
intoxicar / to poison, to intoxicate
el labrador / farmer
largo, larga / long
la lectura / reading
la librería / bookstore
la maleta / valise, suitcase
el mantel / tablecloth
mayor / greater, older
la mesura / moderation
la pala / shovel
el palo / stick, pole
el pan / bread
pasar / to happen, to pass
el pastel / pie; *la pintura al pastel* / pastel painting
pinchar / to puncture, to prick, to pierce
realizar / to achieve (to realize, in the sense of achieving
    something: He realized his dreams, his dreams came true)
recordar / to remember
el resfriado / common cold (illness)
restar / to deduct, to subtract
sano, sana / healthy
soportar / to tolerate, to bear, to endure, to support
suceder / to happen, to come about, to succeed (follow)
el suceso / event, happening
la tabla / board, plank, table of contents
la tinta / ink, tint
la trampa / trap, snare, cheat, trick
tu / your
tú / you
el vaso / drinking glass

Habitat for Humanity®

Allen Rosman

conjunctions

19. ~~By~~ B (? 7.5-3 ✓
20. B ✓ } ? 7.5-2
21. A ✓) 7.5-1
22 ? . ✓ 8.1
23 D ✓
24 B ✓
25 B ✓
26. A ? ✓ 9.5-3
27 C ? w ✓ 4
28 D ? ✓ 10.1
29. de ? ✓
30. que ? ✓
31. ¡Que ~~buena~~ bonita! ✓ "4!
32. Qué fácil es ✓ 4
33. Qué libro interesante "4
34. D ✓
35. C ✓
36 A ✓
37. D ✓
38. D ? ✓ 13.6
39. ·B ✓
40. ~~son~~ el cinco y diez ✓ 14
41. son es el cino, 14
42. ~~son~~ el seis menos cuarto 9 ✓
43. C ✓
44. B ✓

LET'S REVIEW

Test Yourself

§1.
PRONOUNC-
ING SPANISH
SOUNDS

Choose the correct answer by circling the letter.

1. The vowel *a* in the Spanish word *la* is pronounced similarly as in the English word
   A. ate   B. father   C. way   D. April

2. The vowel *e* in the Spanish word *le* is pronounced similarly as in the English word
   A. week   B. ate   C. see   D. father

3. The vowel *u* in the Spanish word *tu* is pronounced similarly as in the English word
   A. cup   B. cute   C. too   D. pudding

4. In Spanish, the letter *g* in front of the vowels *e* or *i* is pronounced as the underlined letter in the English word
   A. help   B. jet   C. go   D. argue

5. In Spanish, the letter *g* in front of the vowels *a, o,* or *u* is pronounced as the underlined letter in the English word
   A. game   B. garage   C. juice   D. gem

6. The letter *h* in a Spanish word, as in *hermano,* is
   A. always pronounced   B. sometimes pronounced
   C. rarely pronounced   D. not pronounced

7. Two vowels together, as in the Spanish word *Europa,* are pronounced separately and they are considered to be a
   A. pure vowel   B. diphthong   C. triphthong
   D. consonant

8. The letter *ñ* in a Spanish word, as in *niño,* is pronounced similarly as in the English word
   A. no   B. canon   C. onion   D. knowledge

9. The double *ll* in a Spanish word, as in *llamo,* is pronounced similarly as in the English word
   A. hello   B. lame   C. yes   D. million

10. The letter *d* in a Spanish word, as in *dar,* is pronounced similarly as in the English word
    A. dare   B. thin   C. dad   D. the

167

§2. CAPITALIZATION, PUNCTUATION, SYLLABLES

I. Divide the following Spanish words into syllables.

EXAMPLE: *hermano   her – ma – no*

1. *eso* _____
2. *mucho* _____
3. *caballo* _____
4. *perro* _____
5. *hermana* _____
6. *aprendo* _____
7. *instituto* _____
8. *comprender* _____
9. *aeroplano* _____
10. *huevo* _____

II. In English, state the simple rule regarding stress when pronouncing a Spanish word. _____
_____
_____
_____
_____

III. In pronouncing a Spanish word, if the word ends in a vowel, *n* or *s,* raise your voice on the vowel in the _____ syllable of the word.

IV. Stressing a vowel means _____ your voice on that vowel.

V. Match the Spanish words designating punctuation marks with the English equivalent.

1. *apóstrofo*
2. *comillas*
3. *paréntesis*
4. *principio de interrogación*
5. *fin de interrogación*
6. *punto*
7. *coma*
8. *punto y coma*
9. *dos puntos*
10. *puntos suspensivos*

_____ period
_____ colon
_____ comma
_____ apostrophe
_____ ellipses
_____ quotation marks
_____ semicolon
_____ parentheses
_____ beginning question mark
_____ final question mark

§3. NOUNS

I. On the line in front of each of the following nouns, indicate the gender of the noun by writing *el* if masculine or *la* if feminine.

EXAMPLE: <u>*la*</u> *madre*

1. ___ *chico*
2. ___ *chica*
3. ___ *tío*
4. ___ *tía*
5. ___ *vaca*
6. ___ *toro*
7. ___ *lección*
8. ___ *ciudad*
9. ___ *costumbre*

10. __ *alumno*	14. __ *gente*	18. __ *día*
11. __ *alumna*	15. __ *coche*	19. __ *clima*
12. __ *estudiante*	16. __ *mano*	20. __ *aire*
13. __ *leche*	17. __ *foto*	21. __ *paraguas*

II. Write the Spanish for each of the following.

1. a history class _____
2. a gold watch _____
3. a little drinking glass _____
4. a darling little dog _____
5. a dear old granny _____
6. a coffee cup _____

III. Write the Spanish word with its definite article for what is requested; for example, *el campo.*

1. The Spanish word for country where you find farmlands as opposed to life in a city is _____.
2. The.Spanish word for country which is a synonym of nation is _____.
3. The Spanish word for country in the same sense as native land is _____.
4. The Spanish word for time referring to the hour on a clock or watch is _____.
5. The Spanish word for time referring to a vague or indefinite duration of time is _____.
6. The Spanish noun used to express the weather is

_____.

7. The Spanish noun for time in the sense of occasions or different times (the first time, the last time) is

_____.

IV. Write, in Spanish, the plural for each of the following nouns.

EXAMPLE: *el chico* __*los chicos*__

1. *la chica* _____	11. *el francés* _____
2. *el dentista* _____	12. *el país* _____
3. *la dentista* _____	13. *el tocadiscos* _____
4. *el profesor* _____	14. *el sacapuntas* _____
5. *la profesora* _____	15. *el paraguas* _____
6. *la flor* _____	16. *el lunes* _____
7. *el lápiz* _____	17. *el martes* _____
8. *la luz* _____	18. *el mes* _____
9. *la lección* _____	19. *el abrelatas* _____
10. *la ilusión* _____	20. *el joven* _____

§4.
ARTICLES

1. Write the four forms in Spanish for the definite article masculine singular and plural and for the feminine singular and plural. _____

2. Write the four forms in Spanish for the indefinite article masculine singular and plural and for the feminine singular and plural. _____

3. On the blank line, write the Spanish word for the indefinite article.

   EXAMPLE: _un_ libro.

   A. _____ naranja   C. _____ platos
   B. _____ libro   D. _____ casas

4. On the blank line, write the Spanish word for the definite article.

   EXAMPLE: _el_ libro.

   A. _____ cuaderno   C. _____ profesoras
   B. _____ señores   D. _____ ciudad

5. When the preposition *a* is in front of the definite article *el,* it contracts to _____ , as in *Voy _____ cine* / I'm going to the movies.

6. When the preposition *de* is in front of the definite article *el,* it contracts to _____ , as in *Vengo _____ cine.* / I'm coming from the movies.

7. Write the Spanish for each of the following.

   A. John's book _____
   B. John's and Mary's books _____
   C. the United States _____
   D. the women's children _____
   E. It's one o'clock. No! It's two o'clock. _____
      _____
   F. the girl's notebooks _____
   G. the boy's little dog _____
   H. What a book! _____
   I. I like coffee. _____
   J. I speak Spanish. _____
   K. El Greco's paintings _____
   L. The little girl's doll _____
   M. Seeing is believing. _____
   N. I am writing in Spanish. _____
   O. I see how easy it is. _____

§5.
ADJECTIVES

I. Complete the following statements or questions by selecting the correct missing adjective and circle the letter of your choice.

1. ¿Es _____ la profesora de español?
   A. inteligente   B. alto   C. español
   D. gran

2. Esta pregunta es
   A. difícil   B. trabajadora   C. fáciles
   D. cada

3. Roberto, Felipe y Marta están
   A. cansados   B. cansado   C. cansadas
   D. cansada

4. ¿Le gusta a usted _____ bicicleta?
   A. este   B. esto   C. esta   D. ésta

5. ¿_____ día es hoy?
   A. cuál   B. qué   C. cuáles   D. este

II. Several words in one word. Using the letters in the word ESPAÑA, how many Spanish words can you write? Write four words at least.

> ### E S P A Ñ A

1. _____   3. _____
2. _____   4. _____

III. Write the Spanish for each of the following.

1. a tall, handsome man. _____
2. a tall, beautiful and intelligent woman _____
   _____
3. one house _____; some boys _____;
   many times _____

IV. Match the following.

1. this book   _____ esos libros
2. these books   _____ aquel libro
3. that book   _____ estos libros
4. those books   _____ ese libro
5. that book (farther away or   _____ aquellos libros
   out of sight)   _____ este libro
6. those books (farther away or
   out of sight)

V. Each of the following sentences contains a blank. From the four choices given, select the one that can be inserted in the blank to form a grammatically correct sentence and circle the letter of your choice.

1. ¿Conoce Ud. a _____ amigas?
   A. *mía*   B. *mías*   C. *mi*   D. *mis*

2. _____ alumno no oye nada porque es sordo.
   A. *Esta*   B. *Ésta*   C. *Aquel*   D. *Esto*

3. María es tan _____ como Roberto.
   A. *alto*   B. *alta*   C. *altos*   D. *altas*

4. ¡Hola, amigo _____! ¿Qué tal?
   A. *mi*   B. *mío*   C. *mis*   D. *mía*

5. Estos libros son _____.
   A. *las mías*   B. *míos*   C. *mías*   D. *mis*

§6. PRONOUNS

I. Several words in one word. Using the letters in the word *PRONOMBRE,* how many Spanish words can you write? Write six words at least.

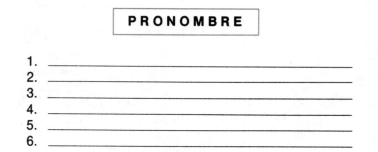

```
PRONOMBRE
```

1. _____
2. _____
3. _____
4. _____
5. _____
6. _____

II. Underline the subject pronouns in the following paragraph.

Pablo, José y yo somos amigos. Cuando nosotros vamos a la escuela, tomamos el autobús y hablamos con las chicas y los chicos. Ellas son muy bonitas e inteligentes.

III. Underline the direct object pronouns in the following paragraph.

    Anoche María y yo fuimos a una fiesta en casa de Ricardo. El padre de Ricardo dijo: "Yo te conozco, María. ¿Me conoces tú?"

    "Sí, sí. Yo le conozco, señor", contestó María. "Mis padres le conocen también. ¿Conoce Ud. a mi amigo José?"

    "Sí, sí. Lo conozco muy bien porque es amigo de mi hijo Ricardo".

IV. Read again the short selection in Spanish in III above. Here, write in Spanish the subject pronouns that you can find in it. _____

_____

V. Each of the following sentences contains a blank. From the four choices given, select the one that can be inserted in the blank to form a grammatically correct sentence and circle the letter of your choice.

1. *¿Está Ud. enfermo? — Sí, _____ estoy.*
   A. *le*   B. *la*   C. *lo*   D. *los*

2. *A mí, _____ gusta el helado.*
   A. *me*   B. *mi*   C. *yo*   D. *le*

3. *A Ricardo, _____ bastan cien dólares.*
   A. *le*   B. *les*   C. *me*   D. *lo*

4. *Juan está _____.*
   A. *lo escribiendo*   B. *escribiéndolo*
   C. *lo escribir*   D. *escribirlo*

5. *María no _____.*
   A. *me lo da*   B. *lo me da*   C. *da me lo*
   D. *me da lo*

6. *Juan quiere _____.*
   A. *me lo dar*   B. *dármelo*   C. *darmelo*
   D. *dar me lo*

7. *Todas las mañanas yo _____ lavo con agua y jabón.*
   A. *se*   B. *me*   C. *nos*   D. *os*

8. *Este regalito es para _____.*
   A. *tí*   B. *ti*   C. *te*   D. *tú*

9. *Me gustan estos guantes y* _____ .
   A. *estos*   B. *éstas*   C. *aquello*   D. *ésos*

10. *¿De quién es este lápiz?—Es* _____ .
    A. *el mío*   B. *lo mío*   C. *mío*   D. *mi*

VI. Complete this crossword puzzle in Spanish.

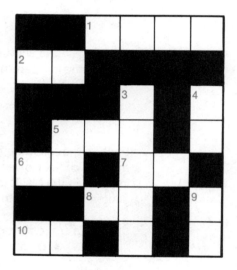

HORIZONTAL:

1. Demonstrative pronoun, feminine, singular
2. Personal pronoun as subject, 1st person, singular
5. Indirect object pronoun, 3d person plural
6. Reflexive pronoun, 3d person, singular and plural
7. Subject pronoun, 2d person, singular
8. Direct and indirect object pronoun, 1st person, singular
10. Direct object pronoun, 3d person, singular, masculine

VERTICAL:

3. Personal pronoun as subject, 3d person, singular
4. Direct object pronoun, 3d person, singular, feminine
5. Indirect object pronoun, 3d person, singular
9. Personal pronoun as subject, 3d person, singular, masculine

§7.
VERBS

I. In the following paragraph, underline the verb forms that are in the preterit tense.

Antes de regresar a su asiento, Juanita vio a un hombre. Cuando Juanita vio al hombre, ella le dijo: "Buenos días, señor". Juanita le dio al hombre su programa y su pluma para escribir su autógrafo. El hombre lo escribió en el programa que Juanita tenía a la mano.

II. The words in the following sentences are scrambled. Unscramble them to find a meaningful sentence and write it on the line provided.

1. *leyendo | está | Pablo | la cocina | en | el periódico.*
   _____

2. *será | Ud. | años | en | diez | rico.* _____
   _____

3. *de Lola | al fin | acepta | Pedro | invitación | la* _____
   _____

III. Complete this acrostic word game in Spanish.

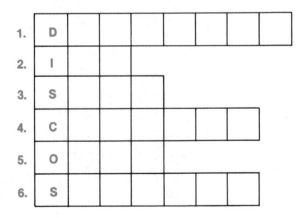

1. D
2. I
3. S
4. C
5. O
6. S

1. Spanish infinitive meaning to return something to someone or to some place.
2. Imperfect indicative of *ir,* 1st and 3d person, singular
3. Preterit tense of *saber,* 1st person, singular
4. Imperfect indicative of *cantar,* 1st and 3d person, singular
5. Present indicative of *oír,* 1st person, singular
6. I gave them *(m.)* to her.

IV. In this acrostic complete each word in Spanish by writing the past participle of the infinitive given for each row.

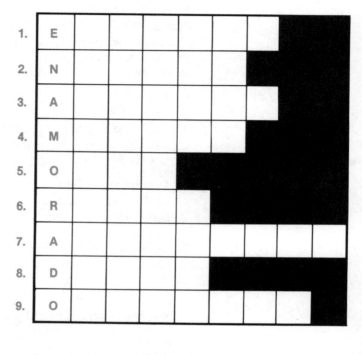

1. *escribir*   4. *morir*   7. *aprender*
2. *nacer*   5. *oír*   8. *decir*
3. *abrir*   6. *reír*   9. *obtener*

§8. ADVERBS

I. Change the following adjectives into adverbs using the *mente* ending in Spanish.

1. *lento* _____   3. *rápido* _____
2. *fácil* _____   4. *feliz* _____

II. Write at least ten common adverbs in Spanish that do not end in *mente*.

1. _____   6. _____
2. _____   7. _____
3. _____   8. _____
4. _____   9. _____
5. _____   10. _____

III. In this dialogue, you and Juanita are talking about the exams in June and summer vacation. Complete the conversation by writing on the blank line an appropriate Spanish adverb from those given here.

bien   rápidamente   recientemente   siempre   también

Juanita: *¿Estás preparado para tus exámenes?*
Usted: *Sí, estoy _____ preparado para mis exámenes.*
Juanita: *Mañana tengo un examen más y luego empiezan las vacaciones.*
Usted: *Los días de vacaciones van a pasar*
_____.
Juanita: *El verano pasado lo pasamos en las montañas.*
Usted: *Mi familia y yo _____ vamos a las montañas.*
Juanita: *En julio hacemos un viaje a Puerto Rico.*
Usted: *Y mi familia y yo _____.*
Juanita: *Voy a mandarte una tarjeta postal desde San Juan si me das tu dirección.*
Usted: *¡Pero yo te di _____ mi dirección! ¿La perdiste?*

IV. Unscramble the following letters to find an adverb in Spanish. Then write the adverb on the line provided.

> **N A C N U** | _____

§9. PREPOSITIONS

I. Match the following.

1. *contra* ___ among, between
2. *hacia*   ___ against
3. *entre*   ___ during
4. *durante* ___ with
5. *con*   ___ toward

II. And match these.

1. *según* ___ without
2. *sin*   ___ on, upon
3. *salvo* ___ after, behind
4. *sobre* ___ according to
5. *tras* ___ except

III. Each of the following sentences contains a blank. From the four choices given, select the preposition that can be inserted in the blank to form a grammatically correct sentence and circle the letter of your choice.

1. *Conozco _____ su hermana Elena.*
   A. *a*   B. *con*   C. *de*
   D. *no preposition needed*

2. *Nuestra profesora de español es muy amable* _____
nosotros.
A. *para*   B. *con*   C. *para con*   D. *por*

3. *Usted habla español muy bien* _____ *ser norteameri-cano.*
A. *por*   B. *para*   C. *con*   D. *de*

4. *Esta taza es* _____ *café.*
A. *por*   B. *a*   C. *para*   D. *al*

5. *Estudio* _____ *llegar a ser médico.*
A. *por*   B. *para*   C. *a*   D. *con*

§10.
CONJUNCTIONS

I. In the following paragraph underline all the conjunctions that you find and write them on the lines provided.

> *Yo no puedo ir a la fiesta en casa de Elena esta noche porque tengo muchas tareas y, como mi madre está enferma, debo quedarme en casa; pero mañana es posible o dentro de tres días.*

_____

_____

II. Complete the following conjunctions by writing on the blank line the Spanish word that is missing.

1. *A fin* _____ *que* / so that, in order that
2. *a menos* _____ / unless
3. *como* _____ / as if
4. *para* _____ / in order that, so that
5. *sin* _____ / nevertheless, however (in whatever way)

III. On the blank line write either *pero, sino* or *sino que,* whichever is appropriate to mean "but" or "but rather."

1. *Me gustaría venir a tu casa esta noche* _____
no puedo.
2. *Pedro no es pequeño* _____ *alto.*
3. *Mi coche no es amarillo* _____ *blanco.*
4. *Pablo no alquiló el automóvil* _____ *lo compró.*
5. *María no conoce al niño* _____ *le habla.*

IV. Five conjunctions in Spanish are hidden in this clock: one conjunction from 12 to 6; one at 3; one at 6; another from 7 to 10; and one at 11. Note that the same letter can be common to the one that follows. This clock has no hands. It's a word clock! Write the missing letters on the lines.

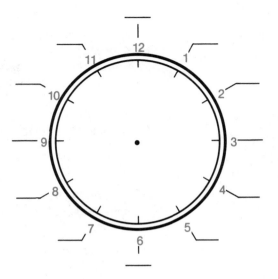

From 12 to 6 write the Spanish for the conjunction "but
rather that."
At 3 write the Spanish for the conjunction "or."
At 6 write the Spanish for the conjunction "and" when
y cannot be used.
From 7 to 10, write the Spanish for the conjunction "but."
At 11, write the Spanish for the conjunction "and"
when *e* cannot be used.

§11.
EXCLAMATORY
STATEMENTS

I. Match the following.

1. *¡Qué clase!*	_____ What a day!
2. *¡Qué alumno!*	_____ What a pupil!
3. *¡Qué idea!*	_____ What an idea!
4. *¡Tal idea!*	_____ What a test!
5. *¡Qué chica tan bonita!*	_____ Such an idea!
	_____ What a pretty girl!
6. *¡Qué libro más interesante!*	_____ What a class!
	_____ How difficult it is!
7. *¡Qué difícil es!*	_____ How easy it is!
8. *¡Qué fácil es!*	_____ What an interesting book!
9. *¡Qué día!*	
10. *¡Qué prueba!*	

§12.
IDIOMS

I. Each of the following sentences contains a blank. From the four choices given, select the one that can be inserted in the blank to form a grammatically correct sentence and circle the letter of your choice.

1. ¿Cuánto tiempo _____ que Ud. estudia español?
   A. hay   B. hace   C. cuando   D. es

2. Hace un año _____ estudio español.
   A. yo   B. como   C. ese   D. que

3. ¿Cuánto tiempo _____ que Ud. hablaba cuando yo entré en la sala de clase?
   A. hace   B. hacía   C. hay   D. es

4. Hacía una hora que yo _____ cuando Ud. entró en la sala de clase.
   A. hablo   B. estoy hablando   C. hablaba
   D. hablé

5. ¿Cuántas moscas _____ en la sopa?
   A. hace   B. hacen   C. hay   D. hacía

II. For each of the following common idiomatic expressions, write in Spanish on the blank line the missing word or words in order to complete them. Choose from among the following: *a, a la, al, con, dar, darse, de, en, estar, hacer, hacerse, hasta, para, poco, por, ser, tener, una, unas, y.*

1. _____ menudo
2. _____ izquierda
3. _____ día siguiente
4. _____ rumbo a
5. _____ la hora
6. _____ prisa
7. acabar _____ + infinitive
8. de hoy _____ ocho días
9. _____ a punto de + infinitive
10. _____ un viaje

11. _____ daño
12. _____ luego
13. _____ mí
14. por _____
15. _____ avión
16. _____ aficionado a
17. _____ dolor de cabeza
18. _____ vez
19. _____ veces
20. un billete de ida _____ vuelta

§13.
DATES,
DAYS,
MONTHS,
SEASONS

I. Each of the following sentences contains a blank. From the four choices given, select the one that can be inserted in the blank to form a sensible and grammatically correct sentence and circle the letter of your choice.

1. ¿Cuál es la fecha? — Hoy es el _____ de enero.
   A. un   B. uno   C. primer   D. primero

2. ¿A cuántos estamos hoy? — Estamos _____ cinco de abril.
   A. por   B. a   C. el   D. la

3. Los días de la semana son domingo, lunes, martes, miércoles, jueves, viernes, y _____.
   A. sabado   B. sábado   C. enero   D. marzo

4. Hay _____ estaciones en el año.
   A. cinco   B. cuatro   C. cuarto   D. tres

5. Generalmente, en Nueva York hace frío en

   _____.
   A. el verano   B. el invierno   C. la primavera
   D. el otoño

§14.
TELLING TIME

I. Study the clocks and underneath each clock write on the blank line in Spanish words the time that is given.

A.

B.

C.

_____   _____   _____

D.

E.

F.

_____   _____   _____

II. Answer the following questions in Spanish.

1. ¿A qué hora va Ud. a la clase de español? _____
   _____

2. ¿A qué hora toma Ud. el almuerzo? _____
   _____

3. ¿A qué hora toma Ud. el autobús para ir a la escuela?

_____

4. ¿A qué hora se acuesta Ud. por lo general? _____

_____

5. ¿Qué hora era cuando sus padres llegaron a casa? __

_____

§15. WEATHER EXPRESSIONS

I. Read the statement in English and select the correct equivalent in Spanish by drawing a circle around the letter of your choice.

1. What's the weather like today?
   A. ¿Hace buen tiempo hoy?   B. ¿Hace calor hoy?
   C. ¿Qué tiempo hace hoy?   D. ¿Qué hora es?

2. It's very warm today.
   A. Hace calor hoy.   B. Hace mucho frío hoy.
   C. Hace fresco hoy.   D. Hace mucho calor hoy.

3. It's foggy this morning.
   A. Hay polvo esta mañana.
   B. Hay neblina esta noche.
   C. Hay neblina esta mañana.
   D. Está nevando esta mañana.

4. Do you like rain?
   A. ¿Le gusta a usted el helado?
   B. ¿Le gusta a usted la nieve?
   C. ¿Le gustan a usted la nieve y la lluvia?
   D. ¿Le gusta a usted la lluvia?

5. Is there much snow here in winter?
   A. ¿Hay mucha lluvia aquí en la primavera?
   B. ¿Hay lodo aquí en el verano?
   C. ¿Hay mucha nieve aquí en el invierno?
   D. ¿Hace mucho sol aquí en el verano?

6. The stars are shining.
   A. Hay neblina y polvo.   B. Hace mucho viento.
   C. Hace mal tiempo hoy.   D. Las estrellas brillan.

7. It's raining now.
   A. Está nevando ahora.   B. Está lloviendo ahora.
   C. Esta mañana llovía.   D. No está lloviendo.

8. It was very foggy this morning.
   A. Había mucho polvo esta mañana.
   B. Había neblina esta mañana.
   C. Hay mucha neblina esta mañana.
   D. Había mucha neblina esta mañana.

9. There was moonlight yesterday evening.
   A. *Hay luna esta noche.*
   B. *Había mucho polvo ayer por la noche.*
   C. *Hay polvo esta noche.*
   D. *Había luna ayer por la noche.*

10. It was snowing when I woke up.
    A. *Estaba lloviendo cuando me desperté.*
    B. *Estaba nevando cuando usted se despertó.*
    C. *Estaba lloviendo cuando usted se despertó.*
    D. *Estaba nevando cuando me desperté.*

§16. NUMBERS

I. Each of the following sentences contains a blank. From the four choices given, select the one that can be inserted in the blank to form a sensible and grammatically correct sentence and circle the letter of your choice.

1. *Dos _____ tres son cinco.*
   A. *menos*   B. *por*   C. *y*   D. *dividido por*

2. *Diez _____ cuatro son seis.*
   A. *por*   B. *y*   C. *dividido por*   D. *menos*

3. *Cinco _____ seis son treinta.*
   A. *y*   B. *por*   C. *dividido por*   D. *menos*

4. *Veinte _____ diez son dos.*
   A. *menos*   B. *por*   C. *y*   D. *dividido por*

II. Match the following ordinal numbers.

1. *décimo*	_____	fifth
2. *cuarto*	_____	ninth
3. *sexto*	_____	eighth
4. *quinto*	_____	fourth
5. *noveno*	_____	sixth
6. *octavo*	_____	tenth

§17. SYNONYMS

I. Match the following synonyms.

1. *acercarse (a)*	_____	*viejo*
2. *acordarse (de)*	_____	*mozo*
3. *alabar*	_____	*caminar*
4. *alimento*	_____	*elogiar*
5. *alumno*	_____	*cocer, guisar*
6. *antiguo*	_____	*estudiante*
7. *andar*	_____	*comida*
8. *camarero*	_____	*recordar*
9. *cocinar*	_____	*aproximarse (a)*
10. *feliz*	_____	*alegre*

II. Read the synonyms in English and select the correct equivalent in Spanish by drawing a circle around the letter of your choice.

1. to cross
   A. *cruzar, atravesar*
   B. *comenzar, empezar*
   C. *comprender, entender*
   D. *contestar, responder*

2. jest, joke, fun
   A. *camarero, mozo*
   B. *chiste, chanza, broma*
   C. *aún, todavía*
   D. *anillo, sortija*

3. to shout, to cry out
   A. *dar voces, gritar*
   B. *dar un paseo, pasearse*
   C. *burlarse de, mofarse de*
   D. *esperar, aguardar*

4. to break
   A. *romper, quebrar*
   B. *rogar, suplicar*
   C. *asombrar, sorprender*
   D. *acabar, concluir*

5. to suffer, to endure
   A. *padecer, sufrir*
   B. *romper, quebrar*
   C. *luchar, pelear*
   D. *mostrar, enseñar*

§18. ANTONYMS

I. Read the words in English that are antonyms in each of the following and select the correct equivalent in Spanish by drawing a circle around the letter of your choice.

1. to be bored / to have a good time
   A. *aburrirse / divertirse*
   B. *apresurarse a / tardar en*
   C. *aparecer / desaparecer*
   D. *olvidarse de / acordarse de*

2. friend / enemy
   A. *bajo, baja / alto, alta*
   B. *amigo, amiga / enemigo, enemiga*
   C. *caro, cara / barato, barata*
   D. *feo, fea / hermoso, hermosa*

3. quickly / slowly
   A. *barato / caro*
   B. *arriba / abajo*
   C. *aquí / allí*
   D. *aprisa / despacio*

4. someone / no one
   A. *algo / nada*
   B. *alguien / nadie*
   C. *alguno / ninguno*
   D. *dentro / fuera*

5. to talk, to speak / to keep silent
   A. *ignorar / saber*
   B. *hablar / callarse*
   C. *maldecir / bendecir*
   D. *negar / otorgar*

II. Match the following antonyms.

1. *llorar* _____ *vaciar*
2. *limpio* _____ *nacer*
3. *llenar* _____ *sucio*
4. *morir* _____ *reír*
5. *amor* _____ *odio*

§19.
COGNATES

I. Alphabet soup. In this word puzzle, find the Spanish words for the English words given below. As you find each one, circle it and check it off the list. The Spanish words are written horizontally, vertically, diagonally.

dormitory, bedroom	correctly
reality	necessary
vocabulary	dentist
photography	city
generous	diary

G	E	N	E	C	I	U	D	A	D	C	O	R	R	E
U	B	C	V	O	A	A	C	L	A	R	I	O	H	L
S	E	C	E	N	D	O	O	V	O	C	A	B	R	Y
D	O	R	M	I	I	T	R	O	M	E	N	T	E	K
C	B	A	L	R	A	L	R	C	A	T	I	C	A	L
Y	X	A	A	Z	O	G	E	N	E	R	O	S	O	U
B	E	I	C	M	N	E	C	E	S	A	R	I	O	E
R	D	E	G	D	E	N	T	I	S	T	A	F	O	T
V	O	C	A	B	U	L	A	R	I	O	F	O	T	O
G	R	U	P	D	O	R	M	I	T	O	R	I	O	P
S	O	L	I	E	L	G	E	N	E	R	A	L	Y	L
I	M	A	G	I	N	A	N	C	I	A	O	E	I	L
D	O	R	M	I	F	O	T	O	G	R	A	F	Í	A
V	O	C	A	B	U	L	E	I	R	O	D	E	A	L

§20. TRICKY WORDS

I. Several words in one word. Using the letters in the word CONSTIPADO, how many Spanish words can you write? Write at least ten.

| CONSTIPADO |

1. ____   3. ____   5. ____   7. ____   9. ____
2. ____   4. ____   6. ____   8. ____   10. ____

II. Match the following tricky Spanish words with their English equivalents.

1. *actual*	____ letter (to mail, post)
2. *la anciana*	____ joke, fun
3. *el bagaje*	____ pregnant
4. *la carta*	____ sand
5. *embarazada*	____ present, of the present time
6. *el éxito*	____ beast of burden
7. *el suceso*	____ drinking glass
8. *la chanza*	____ the old woman
9. *el vaso*	____ success, outcome
10. *la arena*	____ event, happening

Answers

§1. PRONOUNC- ING SPANISH SOUNDS

1. B.	3. C.	5. A.	7. B.	9. C.
2. B.	4. A.	6. D.	8. C.	10. D.

1–10—*see* **§1.**

§2. CAPITALIZA- TION, PUNC- TUATION, SYLLABLES

I.
1. *e–so.*
2. *mu–cho.*
3. *ca–ba–llo.*
4. *pe–rro.*
5. *her–ma–na.*
6. *a–pren–do.*
7. *ins–ti–tu–to.*
8. *com–pren–der.*
9. *a–e–ro–pla–no.*
10. *hue–vo.*

II. If a Spanish word ends in a vowel, the letter *n* or *s*, emphasize the second-to-last syllable of the word.

III. second-to-last.

IV. raising; emphasizing.

V. 6, 9, 7, 1, 10, 2, 8, 3, 4, 5.

I–V—*see* **§2.**

§3. NOUNS

I.
1. *el*		8. *la*		15. *el*
2. *la*		9. *la*		16. *la*
3. *el*		10. *el*		17. *la*
4. *la*		11. *la*		18. *el*
5. *la*		12. *el, la*		19. *el*
6. *el*		13. *la*		20. *el*
7. *la*		14. *la*		21. *el*

1–21—*see* **§3.—3.2.**

II.
1. *una clase de historia*
2. *un reloj de oro*
3. *un vasito*
4. *un perrito*
5. *una abuelita*
6. *una taza para café*

1–6—*see* **§3.3, §3.3–1, 3.3–2.**

187

III.   1. *el campo*   3. *la patria*   5. *el tiempo*   7. *la vez*
       2. *la nación*   4. *la hora*   6. *el tiempo*

1–7 — *see* **§3.3–4** and **§3.3–5.**

IV.   1. *las chicas*   11. *los franceses*
      2. *los dentistas*   12. *los países*
      3. *las dentistas*   13. *los tocadiscos*
      4. *los profesores*   14. *los sacapuntas*
      5. *las profesoras*   15. *los paraguas*
      6. *las flores*   16. *los lunes*
      7. *los lápices*   17. *los martes*
      8. *las luces*   18. *los meses*
      9. *las lecciones*   19. *los abrelatas*
   10. *las ilusiones*   20. *los jóvenes*

1–20 — *see* **§3., §3.1, §3.2.**

§4.
ARTICLES

1. *el, los, la, las* — *see* **§4.1.**
2. *un, unos, una, unas* — *see* **§4.2.**
3. A. *una*   B. *un*   C. *unos*   D. *unas*
   see **§4.2–§4.2–2.**
4. A. *el*   B. *los*   C. *las*   D. *la* — *see* **§4.1–§4.1–2.**
5. *al; al* — *see* **§4.1.**
6. *del; del* — *see* **§4.1.**
7. A. *el libro de Juan* — *see* **§4.1–1.**
   B. *los libros de Juan y de María* — *see* **§4.1–1.**
   C. *los Estados Unidos* — *see* **§4.1–1.**
   D. *los niños de las mujeres* — *see* **§4.1–1.**
   E. *Es la una. ¡No! Son las dos.* — *see* **§4.1–1.**
   F. *los cuadernos de la chica (de la muchacha)* — *see* **§4.1–1.**
   G. *el perrito del chico (del muchacho)* — *see* **§4.1–1.**
   H. *¡Qué libro!* — *see* **§4.2–2.**
   I. *Me gusta el café.* — *see* **§4.1–1.**
   J. *Hablo español.* — *see* **§4.1–2.**
   K. *Los cuadros de El Greco* — *see* **§4.1.**
   L. *la muñeca de la chiquita* — *see* **§4.1–1.**
   M. *Ver es creer.* — *see* **§4.1–1.**
   N. *Estoy escribiendo en español.* — *see* **§4.1–2.**
   O. *Veo lo fácil que es.* — *see* **§4.3.**

§5.
ADJECTIVES

I.   1. A — *see* **§5.1.**
     2. A — *see* **§5.1.**
     3. A — *see* **§5.3.**
     4. C — *see* **§5.4–3.**
     5. B — *see* **§5.4–5.**

II. 1. *es*   2. *se*   3. *esa*   4. *ésa*

III. 1. *un hombre alto y hermoso*—*see* **§5.4–1**
2. *una mujer alta, hermosa e inteligente*—*see* **§5.4–1** and **§10.2–4** to find out when to use *y* or *e*, either of which means *and*.
3. *una casa; algunos muchachos (chicos); muchas veces*—*see* **§5.4–2**.

IV. 4, 5, 2, 3, 6, 1—*see* **§5.4–3**.

V. 1. D—*see* **§5.4–4**.
2. C—*see* **§5.4–3**.
3. B—*see* **§5.6–1**.
4. B—*see* **§5.4–4**.
5. B—*see* **§5.4–4**.

§6. PRONOUNS

I. 1. *no*   3. *me*   5. *pone*
   2. *nombre*   4. *por*   6. *poner*

II. *yo, nosotros, ellas*—*see* **§6.1–1**.

III. *te, me, le, lo*—*see* **§6.1–2**.

IV. *yo, tú, Ud.* —*see* **§6.1–1**.

V. 1. C—*see* **§6.1–2**.   6. B—*see* **§6.1–5**.
   2. A—*see* **§6.1–3**.   7. B—*see* **§6.1–6**.
   3. A—*see* **§6.1–3**.   8. B—*see* **§6.2**.
   4. B—*see* **§6.1–4**.   9. D—*see* **§6.3**.
   5. A—*see* **§6.1–5**.   10. C—*see* **§6.4–1**.

VI.

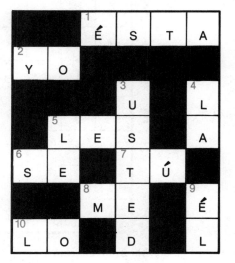

§7.
VERBS

I. *vio, dijo, dio, escribió. see* **§7.5 – 3** and **§7.7 – 3.**

II. 1. *Pablo está leyendo el periódico en la cocina. see* **§7.3 – 2** and **§7.5 – 15.**
   2. *En diez años Ud. será rico. see* **§7.5 – 4, §7.7 – 8,** and **§7.9.**
   3. *Al fin, Pedro acepta la invitación de Lola. see* **§7.5 – 1, §7.7 – 1,** and **§12.2** expressions with *al*

III.

1.	D	E	V	O	L	V	E	R
2.	I	B	A					
3.	S	U	P	E				
4.	C	A	N	T	A	B	A	
5.	O	I	G	O				
6.	S	E	L	O	S	D	I	

see **§7.5 – 1, §7.7 – 1, §7.5 – 2, §7.7 – 2, §7.5 – 3, §7.6 – 18, §7.7 – 3, §7.7 – 8, §7.9,** and **§6.1 – 5.**

IV.

1.	E	S	C	R	I	T	O		
2.	N	A	C	I	D	O			
3.	A	B	I	E	R	T	O		
4.	M	U	E	R	T	O			
5.	O	Í	D	O					
6.	R	E	Í	D	O				
7.	A	P	R	E	N	D	I	D	O
8.	D	I	C	H	O				
9.	O	B	T	E	N	I	D	O	

see **§7.3 – 1.**

§8.
ADVERBS

I. 1. *lentamente* 2. *fácilmente* 3. *rápidamente*
    4. *felizmente—see* **§8.1.**

II. 1. *abajo, arriba, bien, mal, hoy, mañana, siempre,
        nunca, aquí, allí—see* **§8.1.**

III. *bien, rápidamente, siempre, también, recientemente—
     see* **§8.–§8.5.**

IV. *NUNCA—see* **§8.1.**

§9.
PREPOSITIONS

I. 3, 1, 4, 5, 2   II. 2, 4, 5, 1, 3

I and II—*see* **§9.1.**

III. 1. A—*see* **§9.5–1.**
     2. C—*see* **§9.5–2.**
     3. B—*see* **§9.5–3.**
     4. C—*see* **§9.5–3.**
     5. B—*see* **§9.5–3.**

§10.
CONJUNCTIONS

I. *porque, y, como, pero, o—see* **§10.1.**

II. 1. *de* 2. *que* 3. *si* 4. *que*
    5. *embargo—see* **§10.1.**

III. 1. *pero* 2. *sino* 3. *sino* 4. *sino que*
     5. *pero—see* **§10.2–1.**

IV.

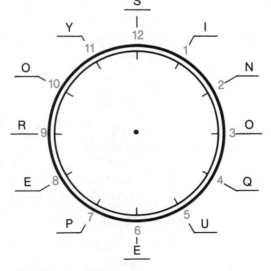

see **§10.2–1—§10.2–4.**

§11.
EXCLAMATORY
STATEMENTS

I. 9, 2, 3, 10, 4, 5, 1, 7, 8, 6—*see* **§11.**

§12.
IDIOMS

I. 1. B—*see* **§12.1.**
2. D—*see* **§12.1.**
3. B—*see* **§12.1.**
4. C—*see* **§12.1.**
5. C—*see* **§12.1.**

II. 1. *a*   2. *a la*   3. *al*   4. *con*   5. *dar*
6. *darse*   7. *de*   8. *en*   9. *estar*
10. *hacer*   11. *hacerse*   12. *hasta*
13. *para*   14. *poco*   15. *por*   16. *ser*
17. *tener*   18. *una*   19. *unas (muchas, varias)*
20. *y*—*see* **§12.2,** common expressions using certain
key words.

§13.
DATES, DAYS,
MONTHS,
SEASONS

I. 1. D—*see* **§13.1.**
2. B—*see* **§13.1.**
3. B—*see* **§13.2.**
4. B—*see* **§13.4** and **§16.1** and **§16.2.**
5. B—*see* **§13.4.**

§14.
TELLING TIME

I.

A. *Son las cinco y diez.*

B. *Es la una.*

C. *Son las seis menos cuarto.*

D. *Son las siete y media.*

E. *Son las once y cuarto.*

F. *Son las cuatro y cuarto.*

see **§14.1—§14.2.**

II. 1. *Voy a la clase de español a las dos y veinte.*—*see*
§14.1.
2. *Tomo el almuerzo a las doce en punto.*—*see* **§14.1.**

3. *Tomo el autobús a las ocho en punto. —see* **§14.1.**
4. *Generalmente (Por lo general), me acuesto a medianoche. —see* **§14.1.**
5. *Eran las dos de la madrugada cuando mis padres llegaron a casa. —see* **§14.1.**

**§15.
WEATHER
EXPRESSIONS**

I. 1. C   2. D   3. C   4. D   5. C
6. D   7. B   8. D   9. D   10. D

**§16.
NUMBERS**

I. 1. C   2. D   3. B   4. D

II. 4, 5, 6, 2, 3, 1

**§17.
SYNONYMS**

I. 6, 8, 7, 3, 9, 5, 4, 2, 1, 10

II. 1. A   2. B   3. A   4. A   5. A

**§18.
ANTONYMS**

I. 1. A   2. B   3. D   4. B   5. B

II. 3, 4, 2, 1, 5

**§19.
COGNATES**

G	E	N	E	C	I	U	D	A	D	C	O	R	R	E
U	B	C	V	O	A	A	C	L	A	R	I	O	H	L
S	E	C	E	N	D	O	O	V	O	C	A	B	R	Y
D	O	R	M	I	I	T	R	O	M	E	N	T	E	K
C	B	A	L	R	A	L	R	C	A	T	I	C	A	L
Y	X	A	A	Z	O	G	E	N	E	R	O	S	O	U
B	E	I	C	M	N	E	C	E	S	A	R	I	O	E
R	D	E	G	D	E	N	T	I	S	T	A	F	O	T
V	O	C	A	B	U	L	A	R	I	O	F	O	T	O
G	R	U	P	D	O	R	M	I	T	O	R	I	O	P
S	O	L	I	E	L	G	E	N	E	R	A	L	Y	L
I	M	A	G	I	N	A	N	C	I	A	O	E	I	L
D	O	R	M	I	F	O	T	O	G	R	A	F	Í	A
V	O	C	A	B	U	L	E	I	R	O	D	E	A	L

**§20.
TRICKY
WORDS**

I. 1. *con*   2. *ti*   3. *pan*   4. *no*   5. *da*
6. *si*   7. *sono*   8. *sopa*   9. *dan*   10. *poco*

II. 4, 8, 5, 10, 1, 3, 9, 2, 6, 7

Index

References in this index are to the Brush-Up section, consisting of the Basics, the Parts of Speech, and Special Topics, indicated by the symbol § (section) in front of a numerical decimal system. The abbreviation *ff* means "and the following."

194